*The Stage Directions
Guide to
Publicity*

The Stage Directions Guide to Publicity

Edited by
Stephen Peithman
Neil Offen

HEINEMANN
Portsmouth, NH

HEINEMANN
A division of Reed Elsevier Inc.
361 Hanover Street
Portsmouth, NH 03801–3912
http://www.heinemanndrama.com

Offices and agents throughout the world

LIBRARY OF CONGRESS CATALOGING-IN-PUBLICATION DATA
The stage directions guide to publicity / edited by Stephen
    Peithman and Neil Offen.
        p.   cm.
      ISBN 0-325-00082-4
      1. Theater—Public Relations—United States.   I. Peithman
    Stephen.   II. Offen, Neil.   III. Stage directions (West Sacramento,
    Calif.)
    PN2053.5.S72   1999
    659.2'9792'0973—dc21   98-51139
                                                                       CIP

Editor: Lisa A. Barnett
Production: Abigail M. Heim
Cover design: Barbara Werden
Cover photo: Rob Karosis
Manufacturing: Louise Richardson

Printed in the United States of America on acid-free paper

03   02   01   00   99   DA   2   3   4   5

For all those in front of the lights and behind the scenes
who understand the magic of theater

Contents

Foreword

Without an audience there would be no theater. And without publicity, there would be no audience—or, at best, only a small one. That's why publicity is so important—and why we're focusing an entire volume on the subject.

And it needs to be a full volume because it's important to remember that there is no one right way to handle publicity. Indeed, each season, each show, each special event becomes a new challenge. Effective publicity relies on an entire tool chest of options; you need to understand those options to meet the needs of a specific situation.

With that in mind, the editors of *Stage Directions* magazine have blended our own knowledge of publicity—theatrical and otherwise—with the expertise of marketing, promotions, public relations, and publicity experts in community, regional, and academic theater, as well as in the general nonprofit and corporate communities.

After an overview of the publicity process, the book first focuses on how to set up and organize your publicity effort. It then moves on, step by step, from how to publicize auditions to getting the word out about the final production. Whether you are a one-person publicity office or part of a larger marketing and public relations team, your goal is the same: to increase the size of your audience. We hope *The Stage Directions Guide to Publicity* provides you with the tools you need to unlock the potential of effective publicity.

About Stage Directions *and This Book*

The majority of the material in this book is based on information that first appeared in the pages of *Stage Directions*, the "practical magazine of theater." Since 1988, *Stage Directions* has published articles on a wide variety of subject matter—not only publicity, but also acting and directing, management, scenic and costume design, lighting and special effects, and much more.

During that time, we've taken a close look at almost every aspect of the publicity process. We've put all that advice together in this book, updated and revised as needed, and added introductions that help put the information into perspective.

As we do with our magazine, we'd like to hear your comments on this book, or suggestions for future topics in our expanding library of *Stage Directions* books. Please write to us at: *Stage Directions*, 3101 Poplarwood Court, Suite 310, Raleigh, NC 27604.

Stephen Peithman, Editor-in-Chief
Neil Offen, Editor

The Stage Directions
Guide to
Publicity

Introduction—
Best Foot
Forward

Theater companies focus on productions. That's as it should be. Putting on plays is, after all, your reason for being. It's what you do.

Yet, no matter how well you've designed your season or how well the production is designed, directed, and acted, you can't succeed financially unless you attract audiences (as well as new company members and staff). For that, you need a strong public relations and publicity plan.

In this book, you'll learn how to put together your own plan and how to make use of cost-effective publicity strategies that really work. First, however, let's take a moment to define some terms.

Any information or promotional material that brings a person, company, production, or cause to the notice of the public may be called *publicity* (and usually is). However, many of the activities that may fall to the publicity manager represent a number of separate, although related, activities.

Publicity actually is the tail end of the *marketing* process. While most people think of marketing as promoting and selling, the process actually starts when you begin to choose a play or an entire season of productions. Aside from the artistic reasons for mounting a show, you naturally consider what your audiences want to see. You use your understanding of your audiences' likes and dislikes, and then choose plays with these in mind. Later, when you publicize a show or season, you put this knowledge to use in order to highlight those elements you know will resonate with the audience.

There are many ways to get the word out. You may produce *promotional materials*, such as flyers, brochures, or direct-mail pieces. You may place *advertising* in print, broadcast, or electronic media. You may stage a *promotional event* that links to your current production (e.g., a blood drive hosted by the cast of *Dracula*). You use *media relations* skills in seeking coverage from a local newspaper, or in asking radio and television stations to run public service announcements (PSAs), or to schedule someone from your company on a talk show.

As you'll note from these examples, publicity targets an event—such as the announcement of a season, the opening of a play, or a fundraiser—that is taking place now or in the near future. In each case, your goal is to move your target audience to action. *Public relations* (PR), however, is concerned with creating awareness, understanding, acceptance, good will, and respect for your company. It may (and usually does) generate ticket sales in the long run, but results are of a more general nature—and may not help very much in the short run. PR is a platform on which you build your marketing and publicity activities, and so must be addressed even when you have no show in production.

There are many versions of the following, but it sums up fairly accurately the distinctions among the terms just mentioned:

> If the circus is coming to town and you paint a sign saying "Circus Coming to the Fairground Saturday," that's advertising. If you put the sign on the back of an elephant and walk him into town, that's promotion. If the elephant walks through the mayor's flower bed, that's publicity. If you can get the mayor to laugh about it, that's public relations. If you planned the elephant's walk, that's marketing. And, if you can get the press to publish the story on page one, that's media relations.

Developing a Base

You'll find many excellent promotional strategies in this book. To make the most effective use of them, you'll need to develop a base for your activities. The following five steps are basic to any marketing or public relations work, and most certainly to an effective publicity program:

1. *Identify your audience.* When theater people think of an *audience*, generally they think of the people sitting in theater seats. That certainly is the result we want from good promotion. But *audience* in the sense used in marketing refers to those people who are likely to come to your productions—your potential customers—if they know who you are, what you do, and where you are.

So who *is* your audience and who influences their decisions about you? They may not be the same people. For example, your audience may be young people, but the decision to send them to your theater probably rests with their parents. Parents, however, may be influenced by the opinion of teachers, other parents, or the community in general. Decide which ones you need to influence and in what order of priority. You can't reach everyone, but you must reach those who are most likely to be your audience.

2. *Determine what images or attitudes your target audiences have of you and theater in general.* Are these images or attitudes positive or negative? Are they correct or incorrect?

3. *Establish what image and attitude you want your audience to have about your company.* Do you want to project the image of quiet professionalism? Avant-garde excitement? Elitist or accessible to all? Intellectually challenging or simply fun? Although you may feel like covering all bases, you risk sending mixed messages if you don't shape your company's image around a central idea and follow through with all your marketing, public relations, and publicity.

4. *Once you know what your target audiences think of you and what you want them to think about you, you can focus on strategies that will emphasize the positive images and overcome the negative ones.* Begin writing your public relations plan by setting priorities. Again, you can't spend an equal amount of time or resources on *all* your audiences. Which groups of people, if approached consistently, will deliver the most people to your door? You also need to take a hard look at the resources you can commit to a promotional effort—not only money, but also time and staff. From the strategies described in this book, choose those that get the most results from your target audiences with the least expenditure of resources.

5. *Finally, take action and evaluate the results.* The first step is obvious, but the latter often is overlooked. If a particular promotional method isn't paying off, it's a waste of time and resources. Either fix it or move on to something else.

The Basics

It's been said that word of mouth is the best form of publicity. But that doesn't mean you can't help matters along. We go into detail on a number of specific strategies later in this book, but here's an overview of the basics.

One of the most effective yet least expensive public relations strategies is to make your theater company part of the fabric of its community. Your image will be enhanced greatly if you are perceived as contributing to the growth and well-being of your area, and it will make your publicity more powerful as well. Join the chamber of commerce and service clubs; go to meetings regularly and get to know the movers and shakers in your town. This will help not only with word-of-mouth publicity, but also for fundraising projects later on.

You also can build on contacts made through these organizations for special promotions, such as flyers distributed at cash registers. You may make friends with a local printer, who might give you a discount on producing promotional materials. You're likely to meet the editor of the local paper or the manager of a radio or television station. Building contacts in the community pays big dividends in your marketing and publicity efforts.

Take part in your local arts organization (or help start one), either as an active member or as a consultant. Contact your local school district to see if someone from your company can share his or her expertise about theater. Most schools are strapped for arts funding, and your volunteering will be much appreciated. If you do a good job, you'll spread the word about your theater to young audiences—and their parents.

Perform scenes or songs for service clubs, senior citizens' centers, or church groups, and encourage a local paper or television station to photograph the performance in action. In fact, any time you work with another group, work with the group's leader or publicity person to see what kinds of joint coverage you can get in the local press. Piggybacking in this manner is good for you both.

Image Is Everything

In dealing with both the public and the media, work to develop an image of high quality. Your promotional materials should reflect a company that takes seriously its artistic mission. Start with a professionally designed letterhead and envelope. If you can't afford to have something designed, see if a local printer can put something together for you. A less expensive alternative is an office-supply superstore; these feature low-priced, attractively designed matching letterhead, envelopes, and business cards, for example, as well as invoices, notepads, and other items.

Carry that professional feeling over to all your printed materials—and not just the look, either. Make sure your pieces are clearly written, free of misspellings and other errors. Audiences and editors form opinions quickly, so make sure you present yourself in the best light possible. Work with local printers to upgrade the quality of every printed piece; most have ways of stretching your budget to turn out promotional materials that reflect your seriousness of purpose.

Develop a Plan

If you don't know where you're going, it doesn't make any difference which road you take. In publicity work, however, you must know the desired outcome so you can determine the best way to get there.

To take advantage of the various media or promotional materials that can carry your message to your audiences, you need to create a publicity plan with measurable objectives. *Measurable* means you can gauge the effectiveness of each promotional activity, so you can repeat it if it works and improve or discard it if it doesn't. (See Chapter 9, "Five Time-Wasters," and Chapter 10, "They Look Like Time-Wasters, But . . .")

Determine which activities you'll be using, then lay them out in chronological order in the form of a publicity plan. (See Chapter 1, "Keeping on Track," to find out how.) After each show and season is over, take time to mull over what was successful and what wasn't. What did you do that you want to do again? What could you do better or avoid altogether? Keep a set of notes, organized by activity, and update them on a regular basis. This notebook will be your bible, a handy reference for you or others working on your company's publicity. Eventually, use it to create a publicity handbook for your company.

Brochures

Brochures serve many purposes. A company brochure explains who you are, helps recruit new members, and bolsters fundraising drives. It needs to suggest stability and mirror your company's mission and values. A season brochure, on the other hand, is focused on selling tickets to those particular shows—although it should mirror your mission and values too. In either case, an effective brochure must be brief and easy to read. Don't load it down with everything you can think of to say about your company or productions. Devise a single, powerful message and put it on the cover. Try to summarize the one shining benefit you can provide your audiences. Remember that the best message answers the question, "What's in it for me?" (See Chapter 13, "Brochures: Did You Know?")

In any brochure, use illustrations or photographs, but don't overdo them, particularly on the cover, where one image should dominate. If you use photos or pictures inside, select intriguing ones that tell the reader good things about your company. And always put captions under your photographs—research shows these are often better read than any other part of the text—and make sure the captions state a selling point.

Speaking of photos, make sure you have a recent photo of your company leadership—preferably a professional headshot. You also should have photos of your company in action, onstage, in rehearsal, or in the community to use in brochures or to accompany press releases. You never know when a good publicity opportunity may arise; with photos on hand, you're better prepared to take advantage of it. (You'll find details on producing great photos in Chapter 14, "Catching an Editor's Eye," and Chapter 15, "Worth a Thousand Words.")

Working with the Media

You'll do much better with your publicity when you understand an editor's point of view. Just because *you* think something is important does not mean the editor will share your opinion. (See Chapter 7, "An Editor Is Not an Ad Salesperson.")

Research shows most journalists judge news value based on the following questions: Does the information have any importance to the reading, listening, or viewing public? Is the information unusual or entertaining? Does it have any human interest? Is the material current? If it isn't, is it a new angle on an old story? (Remember, the word *news* means "new.") Stories featuring well-known or prominent people are often attractive to editors; look for ways to include these people in your activities. (See Chapter 24, "What's in a Name? Maybe an Audience.")

Create a one-page background sheet that gives your company name, business address, history, testimonials from critics or community members, a list of community service and volunteer work, and any honors you have received. Include this sheet with any other information you send out to the media or when you provide information to a school or service club. Duplicate it on your company letterhead. (Of course, make sure everything you send out has your company logo, name, address, and phone number. Pieces get separated from one another, and an editor should not have to hunt for a contact name or phone number.) Update the background sheet regularly.

Theater publicists put out a lot of news releases—an 8½ × 11-inch sheet on which you tell an editor about an event or an idea for a story. We explain the details of a good release and provide a sample release in Chapter 4, "The Perfect News Release." The main point to remember, however, is that you are competing with scores of other releases for the editor's attention. A quick glance at the headline and first paragraph will tell an editor whether or not he or she can use your release.

Feature Stories

Most news releases deal with auditions, awards and honors, and current and upcoming productions, but there are other kinds of stories. Editors are always on the lookout for human-interest pieces or feature stories. A chorus of eight female dancers is not unusual, but a baseball team learning ballet steps to enhance their performance in *Damn Yankees* is a different matter altogether. Unlike a news story, which zeros in on the facts, a feature story takes its time, getting inside the personalities and lives of the subjects. Look for unusual circumstances and people within your company. Look for connections, such as an actor who tutors kids in reading or a head usher who's about to celebrate her 80th birthday. Use community involvement to interest editors while you help build your company's image in the community and promote your shows.

Newspapers

While some newspapers have lost readership in recent years, newspapers are still the most cost-effective media outlet for arts-related activities. Most papers have an arts and entertainment calendar, for instance, that will list your production, and many have arts editors whom you can contact regarding feature stories and reviewers. Newspaper ads also work well for many companies, mostly because theatergoers generally are also newspaper-readers.

Newspapers fall into two major categories: metropolitan and community. Metropolitan newspapers target a large readership over a wide area. While they may list your productions, in-depth arts coverage often is confined to large regional companies. Community newspapers, on the other hand, serve small towns or specific areas within a metropolitan region, and are more supportive of local groups and their activities. These are generalities, however; you need to do some research to find out which newspapers in your area will be the focus for your publicity work. Be aware that space is always at a premium in any newspaper. To get your fair share you need to cultivate a relationship with an editor. (See Chapter 3, "Getting Started.")

Television

The needs of television are simple—action. News shows are always in need of short video clips that can be sandwiched into a program to fill time. Always think of the visual possibilities in any of your activities. (Remember those baseball players learning ballet?) Get to know your television assignment editors. Find out what they are looking for—and what they *don't* want. If you have a public-access cable channel, find out what resources are available to you there.

Radio

You can't show costumes or sets on radio, but as a guest on a talk show, a director can advise callers on how to pick a theater program for their children, or a choreographer can give tips on stretching and exercising, or an actor can talk about overcoming stage fright. Listen to local programs and find out the type of guests they like—then see how you can sell yourself to the show's producer in similar fashion.

Advertising

The secret to effective advertising is to match the audience with the publication or station that is most attractive to that audience. Thus, if you want to advertise a children's show, find out where parents of youngsters are most likely to see or hear your message. Those choices would not work for publicizing something like *Equus* or *Angels in America*.

We talk more about ads later but, in general, an effective advertisement must grab the reader's attention, present your message quickly and succinctly, be true and believable (not necessarily the same thing—something may be true but difficult to believe), and produce the results you want.

Mailings

In many companies, the publicity person also handles direct-mail pieces, including season brochures or flyers for a particular production. Even if you don't deal with these directly, you should be involved in the creative process, because you want all materials to send a similar message. Direct mail is the most cost-effective method of advertising when it is sent to people who already have displayed an interest in your productions (your subscriber list, for example, or names added to your lobby guestbook) or theater in general (mailing lists traded with another company or purchased from a local arts agency).

Stay Grounded

Publicity isn't magic. It won't save a company that sets unrealistic goals, doesn't understand the needs of its audience, or fails to deliver a consistently superior product. And it won't generate an audience for a play that no one cares to see. But if you've done your homework, if you know your audience, and have cultivated the media outlets in your area, effective publicity can make a big difference—and it doesn't have to cost a fortune either.

FIRST STEPS

*E*ffective publicity begins at the earliest stages of a production. It begins, in fact, with a plan of attack—creating a publicity calendar and publicizing auditions.

Keeping on Track
Developing a Publicity Calendar

1

*I*n publicity work, organization is everything. Here's a simple way to make sure your publicity and box office work in coordinated fashion: use a schedule template. Simply stated, the template lists all the publicity-related tasks that must be done in the course of any production, week by week.

Start with something like the following, adapting it to the time frame of the production you'll be publicizing, adding or removing tasks to mirror your situation. In this template, "Week 0" begins the day your production opens. In countdown mode, you then work backwards, detailing the tasks that need to be done in any given week, until you have worked back as far as necessary (in this case, nine weeks out). Although our example is designed for publicity and box-office purposes, the template idea can be used for any aspect of production work.

Week 9: BOX OFFICE: Order tickets
PUBLICITY: Auditions
PUBLICITY/BOX OFFICE: Write mailer to patrons

Week 8: PUBLICITY: Send out calendar listings to monthly publications
PUBLICITY/BOX OFFICE: Print mailer

Week 7:   PUBLICITY/BOX OFFICE. Mailer to post office
          BOX OFFICE: Phone message ready

Week 6:   PUBLICITY: Cast announcement out
                    Set up cast photo session
                    PSAs to radio/television
                    Contact reviewers

Week 5:   BOX OFFICE: Start filling orders from mailing

Week 4:   PUBLICITY: Send out story ideas to feature editors
                    Photo session

Week 3:   BOX OFFICE: Tickets go on public sale
          PUBLICITY: Ticket availability
                    Photo session
                    Event-calendar releases out

Week 2:   PUBLICITY: Check to see that reviewers are set
                    Newspaper ads run

Week 1:   PUBLICITY: Check ticket sales and tweak advertising
                    if needed

Week 0:   PUBLICITY: Press kits to box office for reviewers

During: PUBLICITY: Gather copies of all reviews and articles
                    for scrapbook

After: PUBLICITY: Thank-you notes to all reviewers and
                    editors

Once you've created the template, save it so you can customize it for each future production. Thus, "Week 1" might become "April 24," the Monday just before opening, while "Week 2" becomes "April 17," and so on. For the most flexibility, use a word-processing program. (Someone with knowledge of database software could create a form that will take the date of your opening and then automatically insert all the other dates.)

With dates added, the template is now a publicity schedule. A quick glance each week reminds you of what needs to be done, greatly reducing the chances of any task slipping through the cracks.

Good Auditions Need Good Publicity | 2

Most theatrical publicity is naturally directed toward potential ticket-buyers. But for companies large and small, there's also a need to publicize auditions—both internally and externally. Without that publicity, you either won't have enough actors for the roles or the director won't have a sufficient choice of actors who are appropriate for the roles.

Tips to Get the Word Out—and Actors In

A casting notice or audition announcement should be as detailed as you can make it. First, you want performers to be fully prepared so the audition can move along smoothly and efficiently. Second, you're more likely to get the people you need if you make it clear just what you're looking for.

The most complete casting notice should be in your company newsletter or in a flyer mailed to members, local schools, and other theatre companies. Newspapers usually won't print lengthy notices; instead, give a summary of what you need and a contact name and phone number. Your company answering machine may accept one- or three-minute outgoing message cassettes onto which you can record a great deal of information. If you have voice mail, you also can record a lot of information. Be sure to allow for callers to leave a message in case they have questions.

To be truly complete, a casting notice should contain the following 10 elements:

■ *The name or working title of the production and the producing company.* Include the name of the director or person in charge of the actual audition and a phone number to call for more information.

■ *A brief description of the production and how it will be presented* (e.g., in the round, dinner theater, outdoors, and so on). A one-line description of the play is helpful, especially if it's an original or not well known.

■ *A list of characters*, even if you think "everybody" knows the play and the director is casting it traditionally. Be as specific as possible; include gender, age range, and character type.

■ *If appropriate, specify height, hair color, or ethnicity.* If the character sings, give the vocal range. If the character dances, tell what kind of dancing is required. If the director is going to cast a role(s) in a nontraditional manner, say so (for example, if the director is planning a female version of *The Odd Couple*).

■ *An explanation of how you want the performers to prepare.* Should they be ready with a monologue or a scene with a partner? From a classic or modern play? From a comedy or drama? Or will the director conduct cold readings? Will the auditioners be required to sing? If so, is accompaniment provided? What kind of song should they sing? Should it be from the show? What's needed from dancers? Is there any special dress requirement?

■ *The name and address of the audition location.* Give *specific* directions if it's hard to find.

■ *Where rehearsals will be held and for how long*; people may need to check their calendar. Also, tell where and when the actual production will take place and the length of the run.

■ *If you want to do some prescreening, give a phone number* and make sure there is someone—or an answering machine—ready to take the calls. Prescreening gives you the chance to chat with unfamiliar applicants and determine their potential. It also helps them come to the audition better prepared.

■ *If there could be some doubt, state clearly whether pay is involved*—you don't have to say how much. If you're working under a union contract, say which union and contract. Also note whether you're looking for union performers only or for both union and nonunion.

■ *Some audition notices we've seen include a note from the director*, explaining his or her enthusiasm and personal vision of the show. If you've got room, this can add a human face to what many people see as the worst experience in life, short of death by fire.

WORKING WITH THE MEDIA

*M*ost publicity efforts will involve the mass media—newspapers, magazines, radio, television, the Internet, and the World Wide Web. The following strategies apply to all of these media outlets. When you're considering releasing news to the media, ask yourself these questions:

- Is your news unusual?
- Unique?
- Include a different angle?
- Is it timely?
- How are people touched, involved, entertained, or concerned?
- Which people?
- How many?
- Where do they live?
- Are children, animals, the local economy, or the environment involved?
- Will your story help people save money or solve a problem?
- Let them know about a new problem?
- Does your story tie into another story getting lots of publicity right now?
- Is it part of a trend (preferably local)?
- Are famous (or infamous) people involved?

The more news elements you can relate to your story, the more newsworthy it becomes.

3 | *Getting Started*

Professional publicists will tell you the key to getting good coverage in the media is to *establish personal contacts* with editors and reporters. It's the same in publicizing a theater company or a theater company's shows.

Get to know the person in charge of editorial content. In small-town newspapers, this is probably the editor or publisher. In larger city papers, for theater news, this can be the arts, entertainment, or features editor. At a television or radio station, it could be the news or assignment editor, station manager, general manager, or program director.

How do you find out who's in charge? Put together an up-to-date list of media contacts in your area by calling each media outlet and asking for the name and title of the person to whom information should be sent. Make sure you get the correct spelling of the name and a full mailing address. If mail goes to a post office box, get a street address as well, in case you need to deliver something by hand. Pick up the phone and call the person whose name you've gotten. Start up a conversation. Ask them what they are looking for in terms of news and features. They are usually more than willing to assist you, because an informed publicist will make their lives easier later.

Take an editor or station manager to lunch. Establish a rapport with face-to-face contact. After all, aren't *you* more willing to talk with somebody or answer their call after you have met them in person? Put this psychology to work for your publicity tasks as well.

An editor or station manager's job is to know what's going on in the community. If you have something newsworthy to offer, they are more than willing to listen to learn what's going on in your town or county or neighborhood. Find out what's important to them; also listen to what they have to say. They know what their readers or listeners are looking for, so be creative and open-minded. If you work with them, they will be more than willing to work with you.

Be aware, of course, that particularly with big-city newspapers and radio and TV stations, the upper-echelon personnel may not be available to go out to lunch with every potential publicist who calls them. Work your way down the list then, perhaps to the cultural affairs editor or the community reporter. Eventually, you'll find someone who will be interested in listening to what you have to say.

Once you establish a rapport with the right person, what do you do next? You maintain consistent contact with that person and the local media in general by regular phone calls and by sending news releases—directed to that person. Releases keep your name in front of the editor or station manager. They can get you free publicity. Releases may take a little time to do correctly but they are well worth the effort. (See Chapter 4, "The Perfect News Release," for more on writing effective releases.)

Learn to think like media managers to get their attention and respect. First, target your message to the medium that is most interested in your type of story. Television goes for a mass audience. Radio seeks a very tightly focused group, usually by age and gender. Magazines touch a specialized regional readership. Your local paper may go for a very local angle, and often aims at parents and older readers. The media are highly targeted these days and each outlet tries to stake out its own little piece of the audience. Think about which media outlet in your community addresses *your* target audiences.

There are several topics that media managers seem to favor. If you can think of a way to combine your message with one of these topics, you're in good shape.

1. *Is your story trendy?* At any given time, there are certain topics that the media seem to deal with again and again. It may be

reduction of crime, the need for new schools, substance-abuse awareness, or revitalizing the downtown area. Find some way to connect your message to the media's latest trend.

2. *Does your message fit with one of America's cherished beliefs?* We all like to read stories about little guys who make it big, for example, or someone who has overcome adversity.

3. *Does your message tie into a topic of mass interest?* The media frequently do surveys to find out a community's top concerns. The results are almost always the same—crime, kids, schools, roads, employment. The media always cover topics like these.

4. *Can you relate your message to some community problem?* The media love to cover issues that get people worked up—corruption, dishonesty, cover-ups, racism, cronyism, nepotism, and any other -ism you can think of. Perhaps you can position yourself as the good guys taking on an "-ism."

5. *Is your message a reporter's pet topic?* Because of a particular reporter's particular interest, almost anything has a chance of getting in the media (which, perhaps, accounts for some of the strange stuff you see). Consequently, get to know the likes and dislikes of media folks whenever possible. Radio DJs are especially approachable. Stop by the studio of your favorite station with a box of donuts and start a friendship. Your favors may be returned on the air.

The bottom line is to think like the media and to shape your message to fit their needs. Do that and your message has a good chance of being used. Above all, don't let up. While one media manager may not have the slightest interest in your idea, another will welcome you with open arms. The media need fresh stories every day; hang in there and make sure your company is one of those stories.

The Perfect News Release

Think Like an Editor to Get Your Message Out

Y ou've made contact with the editors and reporters and station managers. You know when they see your name and your company name on something, they at least will take a look at it. But what will that something be? Most times, it will be a news release—or, as it's sometimes called, a press release or media release.

A news release is simply an announcement sent to the media, in which you spell out some newsworthy event (such as the announcement of the cast for your upcoming production) and provide enough information for an editor or reporter to construct a story or calendar item. Most books on public relations mention only one type of news release. However, in recent years, editors have become more flexible in what they'll accept.

■ *Standard Release.* This is still the most common type of news release. It's designed primarily to get the facts across in as straightforward a fashion as possible. Editors use this type of release as part of a larger story or as a framework for a short filler piece or calendar item.

■ *Article Release.* This reads like a short article. Busy editors appreciate it and will sometimes use it just as written—as long as you don't come across as overly promotional. A release like this is more likely to find a home in community newspapers, not large metropolitan papers.

- *Tease Release.* As the name implies, this tantalizes the editor with just enough information to get him or her to call you. If done properly, this may lead to an interview, which could result in a complete news or feature article. This is not the type of release a beginner should attempt, however. What strikes the writer as clever may seem amateurish to an editor, and create a bad impression of your theater—and that's something you never want to do.

While theater itself is creative, you can get the most mileage by using the standard release. Remember that its purpose is to give the editor or writer essential facts, with the most important information in the first few paragraphs. If your release announces that tickets are now on sale to the general public, don't make the editor wade through two pages looking for ticket prices or a box-office number. Make it easy for an editor and your news release will pay big rewards. (See the sample release at the end of this chapter.)

There's no great mystery to getting your press releases published. Just get to know the needs of the media outlets, and think like an editor.

1. *Target your press releases.* Most media outlets receive anywhere from 50 to 100 press releases a week, with approximately 10 to 25 percent of those having nothing to do with the publication to which (or editor to whom) they are sent. Read the publication. Get to know what type of articles and press releases it prints. (If you have taken an editor to lunch, you already know what he or she wants.) Gear the release to the media outlet itself—don't expect that the editorial staff will take the time to critique, edit, and print it. It will end up in the trash or recycling bin if it's not in a relatively printable form when it comes in the door.

2. *Make sure your press release is news.* Again, this will depend on the media outlet itself. The local weekly paper may be interested that your board president has been elected to serve on the local arts council, but the editor of a larger publication probably will not be. That editor would be intrigued more by the fact that your ticket sales have increased despite an economic downturn, or that your company has won a national award. Remember, what is news to one publication may be fluff to another.

3. *If you don't have letterhead paper, place your company name and address in the upper left-hand corner of the first page.* The phone

number and name of the contact person (typically the publicity person) is usually in the upper right-hand corner. Remember to include both day and night phone numbers.

4. *Two spaces below, put the release date.* Normally, this will say "FOR IMMEDIATE RELEASE," so the information can be used as soon as it is received. A specific date means the information should not be announced until that time. Such a request occurs when you want all media in your area to announce your news on the same day, or if you want to alert the media of an event before you notify the public.

5. *About one-third of the way down the page, type your headline or title*; this space allows the editor to jot down comments or notes. Use all caps or boldfaced print for the title. If the title is more than one line, single-space it. (The release itself is double-spaced.)

6. *Type the body of the release double-spaced throughout.* There's a good reason for this—it's more readable and, again, you leave room for the editor to make notes or changes. Indent all paragraphs with normal spacing between them. Use 12-point type if possible; avoid fancy typefaces such as script—they are hard to read and irritate editors.

7. *Editors expect releases to follow standard journalistic style, answering the questions "Who?," "What?," "When?," "Where?," and "Why?"* Make sure you give this information in the first sentence or two. For example: "The Poorhouse Players present Neil Simon's *The Odd Couple* at the Jackson Community Theater, June 5 through 12 at 8:15 P.M."

The remainder of the release should explain or elaborate on the first paragraph: ticket prices and where they may be purchased, a phone number for more information, the theater's address, the director's name, lead players' names, and a one-sentence summary of the play's plot or story.

In general, organize your press release as an inverted pyramid, with the most important information stated first. (See the following sample release.) This gives the editor the opportunity to read the first line and see if it's important. Of course, *you* think it's important, but there are just not enough hours in the day for an editor to read every release in its entirety. This is why it is vital that the first lines of your release grab the editor's attention. This, in turn, makes it more likely he or she will read the whole thing—and this, in turn, makes it more likely for it to see print.

Use quotes. They add life to releases. But avoid long-winded quotes from people who are involved only peripherally in the story. Look for comments that are colorful, pithy, and to the point.

8. *If possible, keep releases to one page.* If it runs longer, type "—MORE—" centered at the bottom of the page. This way, if pages become separated, the editor knows there is additional information. Following pages should be identified at the top with a word that indicates the subject matter followed by the page number; for example: "Couple/2."

9. *At the end of the release, type "###" centered*, to signify that there is no more material.

Address your release to someone in particular. There is nothing more telling than if an envelope comes addressed only to "Editor" or "Entertainment Editor." If you do this, you are emphasizing the fact that you are sending it to them and every other media outlet in your area. If you don't show enough interest to make sure it reaches the right person, don't expect that a publication or station will take an interest in what you have to say. (Note: If you have established a rapport with an editor at the outset, this should be no problem.)

Call or write first to tell that particular person you're sending a release. This works to your advantage since the editor will, in all likelihood, pay particular attention to it when he or she receives it. (See Chapter 5, "The 'Be Prepared' Letter.") After it's sent, call again, confirm they have received it, and ask if there are any questions; this will bring your release to the top of the pile. Editors do not mind being called as long as you don't pressure them to run what you've sent.

Find out if releases can be sent by fax or e-mail, and get those numbers or addresses, if needed. If you plan to send your releases via e-mail, use the same format, except for double-spacing, which most e-mail programs won't recognize. It's always a good idea to find out if a reporter or editor wants to receive releases via e-mail— some do, some don't. As always, provide the information in the form that's most likely to please the person who decides whether something is newsworthy.

Don't be mad if the newspaper or radio station does not use your release. It's an editor's job to provide, in that person's estimation, what is important at that particular time. He or she may have determined that something else was more important. Keep sending out those releases, because your news eventually will become more important than someone else's.

A Sample Release

Here's a good example of an effective news release. Note the inverted-pyramid style, with the most important facts at the beginning.

March 17, 1998

FOR IMMEDIATE RELEASE

Media: For further information, please contact Julia Gallagher,

(555) 555-3466

Off-Broadway hit to make Canadian premiere at Berkeley Street

Theater

TORONTO: New York producer Leonard Soloway announced today that off-Broadway's hottest ticket of this past year, *Gross Indecency: The Three Trials of Oscar Wilde*, will make its Canadian premiere in Toronto at the Berkeley Street Theater (Canadian Stage Theater Downstairs at 26 Berkeley Street).

Performances for this summer-long engagement are set to begin on June 8, 1998, with the official opening night on June 25, 1998. Tickets will go on sale Wednesday, March 18, for performances from June 8, 1998, to September 5, 1998. Tickets range in price from $29 to $45. They can be purchased in person at the Canadian Stage Box Office, any TicketMaster location, or by calling TicketMaster at (416) 872-1111 to charge.

Gross Indecency: The Three Trials of Oscar Wilde is the hit play commemorating the 100-year anniversary of Irish playwright Oscar Wilde's release from prison. This critically acclaimed drama chronicles the arrest, judgment, and sentencing of the most celebrated playwright of his time. The production by Moisés Kaufman uses original trial transcripts, letters, and biographies written by Wilde, his contemporaries, and other first-hand sources. The drama focuses on Oscar Wilde as an artist, persecuted as much for his art and radical opinions as for his homosexuality.

Gross Indecency has been heralded by critics across the United States, with productions currently running in New York, San Francisco, and Los Angeles. In New York, the show was completely sold out, with huge waiting lists and lines where hundreds were turned away.

Gross Indecency has been proclaimed "brilliant" by Donald Lyons of the *Wall Street Journal*, "compelling" by Clive Barnes of the *New York Post*, and a "theatrical phenomenon" by Linda Winer of *Newsday*. The play has been named "Best of the Year/Top 10" by *Time* magazine, the Associated Press, *Entertainment Weekly*, and many other publications.

###

The "Be Prepared" Letter | 5

Let Editors Know What's Coming Their Way

*I*f you want to get better results from your publicity, many professional publicists recommend a "be prepared" letter. Here's how it works.

Step 1

Six weeks to a month before an event (whether it's a show, fundraiser, or whatever), send a letter to appropriate editors or radio/television program directors. The letter should be addressed to each by name (avoid the form-letter look) and say something like, "We're the Poorhouse Players, and you'll soon be hearing from us with news about our new production of the new Pulitzer-Prize–winning play, *Moose Murders*. In the meantime, if you have any questions, call us."

Don't be too specific. The idea is to prepare the editor to expect something more from you. That way, when the full information does arrive, he or she will be ready for it. Note that the letter mentioned something newsworthy ("new Pulitzer-Prize–winning play") to help the editor remember.

Be sure your letter lists a contact person and phone number for your organization. Someone might call.

Step 2

A few days later, follow up with another letter, this time with a news release or a press kit. If you have photos, include them.

You might include some ideas for feature stories as well. Talk about appropriate visuals that will interest the editor, such as costumes, unusual staging, or preparation. Remember that still photos and video footage are very different, and plan accordingly.

No matter what you send, always include a short, personalized cover letter addressed to your media contact. A letter always gets more attention than a news release alone. And make sure anything you send is printed cleanly and free of typographical errors or misspellings.

Step 3

Phone the editor or reporter about a week later. Call at an appropriate time. For most newspapers, late morning is good. For television, don't call an hour before a news broadcast—or during, for that matter.

"I sent you a press kit last week," you say. "I just wanted to make sure you received it." If the answer is yes, ask if there is anything you can clarify—and proceed to sell your ideas all over again. If the answer is no, just say, "Then all I'd like to leave you with is . . ." and proceed to sell your ideas one more time!

Reactions will vary, but if the editor shows any interest at all, ask for an interview or whatever it takes. If the editor is unsure, say you'll call back later. Remember, publicity is a sales job. You have to sell the media on your theater and its production. The better prepared you are, the better results you'll get.

Media Relations: Dos and Don'ts

6

Here's What Editors Have to Say

*L*ooking for ways to improve your media-relations program? Consider these suggestions, gathered from editors and public relations professionals.

Do:

■ *Remember that a news release is essentially a direct-mail communication to an editor.* Think about direct-mail pieces you receive and try to make yours tasteful, neat, and to the point. Always consider the image your release presents of your company.

■ *Stick to the facts.*

■ *If the story warrants, call the editor.* Offer additional details, photos, and possible angles for related feature articles. Extra effort can pay off.

■ *Provide a photo whenever possible.* Releases with pictures have a better chance than those without.

■ *Prune your media list to those most likely to run your material.* There's no point in wasting paper and postage.

- *Be clear.* Don't assume extensive knowledge and imagination from readers or editors. Spell it all out and explain where necessary.

- *Before printing your release, have it checked by someone who knows how to proofread and knows the facts.* The recall of a release because of inaccuracies is a pain. Worse, it makes your company look bad.

- *Read local papers to see what releases by others are used.* Try to determine why and tailor your releases accordingly.

- *Always leave room at the top of the first page.* This lets the editor write a new headline and make notes to other editors or writers.

- *You might consider writing two releases, one with more detail.* The detailed one goes to the arts editor; the general one can go to other editors.

Don't:

- *Call the editor and ask when the release will be published.* The editor may not know until the last moment.

- *Write a cover letter that hints at possible advertising if the media outlet runs a story.* Editors are concerned with good editorial coverage. Period. Many will be offended by the notion that their coverage can be bought.

- *Send the same release more than once.* Editors will think you're trying to pull a fast one and may not print anything.

- *Make claims for a production or achievement without supporting evidence or references.*

- *State facts without explaining the importance to the reader.* The essential question to answer is "So what?"

- *Fail to point out that the event is the first of its kind, largest, smallest, or otherwise significant for any reason.* Don't assume the editor or readers know.

- *Claim that a production or company is "unique" or revolutionary unless it truly is.* No puff, please.

- *Send out information until you are ready to answer inquiries.* Otherwise, you will get burned—and the editors and readers will stoke the fire.

- *Try to represent anything old as new.* Play it straight. Editors catch on eventually and, like elephants, they have long memories.

- *Ask to see an item before it runs.*

■ *Send poorly printed releases or press kits.* Releases must be typed and reproduced on a high-quality photocopier. If they can't be read easily, they probably won't be read at all.

■ *Forget to check and double-check numbers, names, and dates.* The most frequent error is the mismatched day and date (for example, Thursday, April 14, when it should be Thursday, April 15, or Wednesday, April 14). Watch it!

7 | *An Editor Is Not an Ad Salesperson*

*A*s noted previously, many editors will be offended at the notion that their coverage of your company can be "bought," that it's advertising for your theater. That's because, at most newspapers and television stations, there is a "church/state" wall between advertising and editorial. (This is frequently less true, however, in radio.) To most editors, therefore, it's extremely important that news stories bear no resemblance to advertising.

Write a News Release as an Article

The sin committed most often by publicity novices is mistaking a news release for an advertisement. In an advertisement, you can say almost anything; in a news story, you can't. To stay on an editor's good side, and get your information printed—and printed correctly—make sure your release contains no sales hyperbole. If you use adjectives, substantiate them by quoting an expert or a reference that can be checked easily. Start with the first paragraph.

Poor:

The Poorhouse Players are pleased to present the hilarious mystery hit, *Arsenic and Old Lace*, June 4–14 at the Veterans Memorial Theater. The outstanding production is

under the capable direction of Alan Parks. Popular actresses

Mary Trump and Helen Everett are featured as the two

murderous Brewster sisters.

What's wrong? To begin with, who cares if *you're* "pleased" or not? The editor certainly doesn't. And just who says the show is "hilarious"? Or that Alan Parks is "capable"? Or that Mary Trump and Helen Everett are "popular"? While all these may be true, the editor is more likely to cut all this out, and what's left is boring. Worse, the editor may substitute his or her own words, which may be neither accurate nor positive. Solution: Write your releases like news stories and see more of them in print.

Better:

The Broadway mystery-comedy hit *Arsenic and Old Lace* opens

June 4 at the Veterans Memorial Theater, and continues

weekends through June 14. Performances for the Poorhouse

Players production begin at 8:00 P.M. Thursday, Friday, and

Saturday, and at 2:00 P.M. on Sunday. Directed by Alan Brewer,

this perennial favorite features Mary Trump and Helen Everett

as the two murderous Brewster sisters.

OK, so it's not Hemingway. But this version is more likely to be used intact. It contains more essential information (days and times). "Broadway hit" can be documented, as can the "perennial favorite." And it begins with a news "peg"—opening night.

And While You're at It . . .

Besides more information for the reader, include anything that will make the event more newsworthy. For example, if this is the area premiere or an unusual production of this play, say so. And as vital as the first or lead paragraph is, the last one or two paragraphs are also important. Close with where to write or call for more information and the address of the theater.

8 | *Make the Most of Public Service Announcements*

*I*n addition to news releases, news stories, and advertising, there are other ways of getting your theater's name in the news or on the air. Here's information on one of the easiest ways to do that.

Tips on PSAs

PSAs are a good way for nonprofit organizations to build public awareness, thanks to the time or space contributed by radio and television stations. Basically, a PSA is free advertising, offered only to nonprofit groups as a community service. However, while they may be free, PSAs are not automatic simply because yours is a nonprofit group. For one thing, there are a lot of people clamoring for air time. Therefore, following a few rules can increase your chance of success in placing PSAs.

First, call each radio and television station in your area and ask for the name of the public-service director; while you're at it, make sure you have the correct address as well. Also find out how far ahead of the event the media outlet needs your information. Transfer this information to the publicity schedule for each production (See "Keeping on Track" in Chapter 1.)

To place PSAs, start with a cover letter on your company's letter-head. Include today's date and your name (or that of another contact person) and phone number in case the station needs more informa-tion. Keep your request brief and to the point, but be sure to give all pertinent information about your organization and its qualifications for public-service coverage. It is essential that every PSA include the full legal name of your company; its address and phone number; plus the name, title, and phone number of your contact person. The stations use this information to show to the Federal Communications Commission.

Each script or letter should provide the length of the spot(s) and the air dates desired. If there is a firm cut-off date, be sure to mention this. Plan your spot lengths carefully, using the following general guidelines:

- 5-second spot: 10 to 12 words; one slide or image
- 10-second spot: 20 to 25 words; two slides or images
- 20-second spot: 40 to 45 words; four slides or images
- 30-second spot: 60 to 70 words; seven slides or images
- 60-second spot: 130 to 150 words; up to 15 slides or images

It's a good idea to read through your PSA several times to see if it flows well. What looks good on paper may not sound as good read aloud. Standard format is to use all capital letters for the portion to be read on the air.

Most radio stations have staff do the taping of your spot. Some television stations may do this, but others will expect you to do the work yourself. However, television PSAs are the most costly to pro-duce and are also more complicated. So, while some stations will donate time and equipment to produce a 15- or 30-second spot, oth-ers may give preference to the ready-made spot, if done well. If so, ask your local public-access cable organization if they can help you produce the spot. Just be sure to check with the television station to find out the kind of production values it requires.

Note that stations usually do not return materials, nor do most acknowledge receiving them. You can ask for tapes back, but don't count on getting them returned. Since stations receive many re-quests for PSA coverage, allow at least six weeks' advance time to get your materials to the public-service director. PSAs sent in or de-livered on shorter notice will very likely not be used. Remember: Ma-terials that are properly addressed and prepared, received well in advance of requested air dates, and show they serve a real commu-nity interest will be given priority for on-air use.

A Sample PSA

FOR IMMEDIATE RELEASE

Poorhouse Players Presents *Tintypes* July 2–16

10-SECOND SPOT

CELEBRATE AMERICA'S MUSICAL HERITAGE WITH *TINTYPES*,
PRESENTED BY THE POORHOUSE PLAYERS, JULY 2nd
THROUGH 16th, AT THE JACKSON COMMUNITY THEATRE. FOR
TICKET INFORMATION, PHONE 555-1212.

15-SECOND SPOT

CELEBRATE AMERICA'S MUSICAL HERITAGE WITH *TINTYPES*,
A DELIGHTFUL AND TUNEFUL PRODUCTION THE WHOLE
FAMILY WILL LOVE, PRESENTED BY THE POORHOUSE
PLAYERS, JULY 2nd THROUGH 16th, AT THE JACKSON
COMMUNITY THEATRE. FOR TICKET INFORMATION, PHONE
555-1212.

Five
Time-Wasters

So far, we've been telling you what to do—how to make contact with editors, how to write an effective news release, how to prepare the ground for a news release—but it's also important to understand what not to do. Otherwise, you risk wasting valuable time and energy on activities that will not provide any appropriate payoff. The trick, of course, is determining which are time-wasters and which are not.

They Seem Like Perfectly Logical Things to Do, But . . .

CHRIS LANING

*T*he time you spend publicizing your theater is one of the best investments your company can make. So it's important to be sure your time and efforts aren't wasted.

Here's a look at several common publicity time-wasters. All of these are activities that *sound* like perfectly logical things to do. After all, lots of other organizations do them. Well-meaning supporters even may encourage you to do them. But don't—even if you have to spend extra time explaining why not. Your time will be better spent doing something more effective, more efficient, and more fun.

1. *Don't send calendar notices to media that don't do calendar notices.* Newspapers and radio stations are subject to the same economic squeeze as everyone else. "Community Bulletin Board" departments, where nonprofits and charities can have events announced for free, are a thing of the past in many areas. Check each paper's or station's policy *before* you send in listings.

Do they have a place to put them? If not, save yourself

the postage, or send your news release to a specific individual, such as the arts reporter, instead. (You then can invite that individual to cover you in person.) In fact, don't send any announcement to a paper you haven't seen without taking a look at a few copies first. (It's considered a bit tactless, by the way, to call a newspaper and ask for a sample issue. That tells them right away you don't subscribe. Remember you're asking them to do you a favor. Go out and buy a copy.)

The same holds true for other media. You need to be sure your news is the kind they're looking for, and that it will reach the audience you're looking for. In other words, don't send everything to everybody. Call and ask what they'd like to see and when.

2. *Stay away from "grip-and-grin" photos.* There are certain kinds of photos where when you've seen one, you've seen 'em all. The leading character in this cast of cliches is the grip-and-grin—Person A shaking Person B's hand, or awarding a plaque, or handing the local charity representative a check. The faces may be different, but the pose, the grins, the suits, and the podium might just as well have come from the prop closet. Newspaper people get pretty bored by these pictures; in fact, some papers won't even print them.

So use some imagination. Present the check, but have Marie Antoinette do it in full costume. Make it a bag of "gold" instead of a check. Thank your benefactor with a moonlight serenade (with photographer). Use a scene shot from your production and give it a new caption ("Alas! Oh, woe! Only three more days left to see [the name of your play]!").

3. *Don't call to ask if they're going to run your story.* Calling the reporter to ask if your article is going to run is a waste of time for one reason: The reporter is not the one who makes that decision, the editor is. Calling the editor to ask the same question interrupts a person who's working on a very tight deadline, and it often comes across as rude and annoying. After all, you're probably not the only person asking the same thing.

The *real* reason you're calling is that you hope to persuade or charm them into it. It almost never works. An editor doesn't want to substitute your news judgment for his or hers. Rather than call and insist that your news is important, put your efforts into showing *why* it's important in the news release itself: why your new production is different and fun; why the new direction your company is taking is exciting. Let it speak for itself, and it will sell itself. This makes for better articles and better media relationships.

If you're calling because you really need to know if your article made it into the paper—for instance, if you need to get several copies immediately to mail out—find out ahead of time when it comes off the press, and when it does, call the front desk. As soon as it has a copy, you'll get the information.

4. *Don't invite coverage of something with no visual potential.* All media outlets, even print media, are visually oriented these days. It's a waste of time to invite reporters to cover something in person if they can't take, or at least imagine, some good pictures. You may think this is easy because, after all, you do theater. But what if your news is about receiving a grant for a new computer? Or open auditions for a production that isn't costumed yet?

Again, a bit of imagination may conjure up a good visual. Perhaps Pierrot can embrace a giant photo of the new computer to show how wonderful it's going to be. Round up your office volunteers, put scripts in their hands, and pose them as a "chorus line" of people pretending to read for a part. You can take photos ahead of time and have prints available if you have the services of a professional photographer (perhaps as a volunteer). But many media people prefer to take their own photos. Be sure to ask them about this ahead of time.

5. *Don't break your back courting television coverage.* This isn't to say you should not keep the local television stations well informed of anything newsworthy you do. Indeed you should, and tell them well ahead of time exactly when and where they can show up to cover it. But don't hold your breath expecting them to show up with rolling cameras every time. Local news and "feature" slots on television are even more besieged with stories than newspapers are, and assignment editors make split-second decisions about where to send the crews, based on such things as the weather, national news, and breaking "disaster" stories—none of which you can control. Your job is to invite the television stations, to be ready with good photo opportunities (absolutely vital) and background information when they do show up, to thank them, and to enjoy the results. If you get a few minutes on the local news station once a year or so, pat yourselves on the back. You're doing well.

10 | *They Look Like Time-Wasters, But...*

... These Seven Activities Actually Do Bring Results

CHRIS LANING

At times, publicizing a theater can be a discouraging task. Although you are working hard, some of the things you do don't seem to have much result. It may seem as though you've been wasting your time. In this situation, the logical thing would be to stop doing these things. However, there are seven seeming time-wasters that can pay off.

1. *Sending a publicity notice when you think it's too late.* Send it anyway, and don't apologize. (At least, not too much.) Sure, it's better to get your information in on time, but perhaps you didn't know when the deadline was, or perhaps unforeseen events intervened. This way, even if the deadline is past, your news release, article, or announcement at least will be there if suddenly a hole needs to be filled. And at worst, you still have reminded someone at your local newspaper, radio, or television station that your company exists and does interesting and worthwhile things. That will help next time. (And next time, make sure you do get them out on time.)

2. *Sending news releases to television stations, even if they never seem to respond.* Local television stations are extremely

busy places. Every day when they put their broadcast together, they never know ahead of time exactly what will happen that day. They have to choose just a few from a multitude of good stories. We cautioned you in the previous chapter against trying too hard to court television stations. But keep sending them your news. While you shouldn't *expect* them to cover everything you do, you never know when you may be their perfect local tie-in to a story on "Arts Funding Cut Everywhere" or "The Magic of Make-Believe." Even if you don't hear from them, they do read what you send them. They're looking for news. Give them your best.

3. *Taking and sending good photos, even if they don't always get used.* Remember that all media, including print media, are visually oriented these days. Sending good photos with your releases gets your people's faces known in the community, and shows (better than telling) that you're out there doing interesting things. Even if they can't use your photos every time, the reporters and editors see them, and believe me, they notice good photography when they see it.

If you can't pay for photography, perhaps you can strike a deal with a professional photographer for volunteer services in return for cost of materials and a little free advertising. Developing a reputation for providing sharp, clear, and witty photos is worth the time you put into it.

4. *Displaying a sense of humor.* Besides making your publicity job a lot more fun, using humor helps your name stick in community members' minds. Don't feel you have to reach for gags. Just loosen up enough to let the natural spoofs and irreverence in your troupe come out. Your job is to ride herd on the humor and pick the things that will add to—not distract from—your message.

5. *Holding press conferences.* If you've had inquiries from several reporters about a particular story, consider inviting them to all come at one time and hear about it. That's all a press conference is. It's an especially helpful way to do things if there are several people the reporters should talk to, since you can have all of them there at once.

Still, don't count on everyone you invite actually coming. (Providing snacks and coffee may help.) Set it up, have plenty of background material ready, but don't exhaust yourself over it. Every reporter who does come gets more and better material than if he or she had just talked to you on the phone, and more good material means more likelihood of a good story. Don't forget to take your own photos and write a good story yourself, while you're at it.

6. *Setting up personal interviews.* There is really no substitute for talking to people face to face. In your job, you are seldom in a position where you can *make* people publicize your organization. Instead, you must persuade them. And most people find it a lot harder to say "no" to someone they know personally. Yes, it takes time, and your time is limited; but use some of it to cultivate your contacts within the community, local papers, and news stations.

Similarly, it's well worth your while to arrange for a reporter to interview people in your organization directly. You can coach them ahead of time about what to say (and not say). But just because you're the PR person, don't feel you have to be the only one giving out all the information. News is freshest straight from the mouths of participants, and if your reporter is any good, interviews will make for a better story.

By the way, think carefully about the facts you give, since you will probably not have a chance to see any article about you or correct any errors before it goes to press. Like it or not, few reporters can give you that opportunity.

7. *Cultivating carefully chosen small markets.* If you've got the major publicity avenues covered, think next about where you can reach out to smaller groups who will be especially interested in what you're doing. If you do a lot of musicals, are all the local music teachers on your mailing list? What about church choir directors? Do the local centers for senior citizens (the "grandparent" market) know about your shows for children? If you do productions with social justice themes, can you get into the newsletters of community groups with that kind of focus? It's hard to measure how many tickets you sell this way—but certainly anytime you have people in the community thinking about you, especially in a positive way, it has to be good.

Media:
Did You Know?

The "Did You Know?" department has been a prominent feature of *Stage Directions* since the magazine's very first issue in 1988. Short items about sundry theatrical subjects gleaned from companies across America, various readings, conversations, and other sources, "Did You Know?" offers a variety of information and perspectives.

The Pay's the Thing

If you live in an area where there are a number of theater companies, you might want to consider talking to your local newspaper about running an article such as the one we saw in a large metropolitan newspaper, the *Sacramento Bee*. Called "The Pay's the Thing," this nearly full-page article listed ten ways in which readers can save money at area theater companies.

The ways include season tickets, group discounts, students and senior discounts, weekday performances, preview performances, pay-what-you-can nights, day-of-performance discounts, discount coupons, dinner theater, and volunteering. The first five are probably obvious; the second five may need some explanation.

A few Sacramento-area theaters offer one performance per production where audience members pay whatever their budget will bear. At the Foothill Theatre Company, it's the last Thursday of every show's run. At the B Street Theatre, it's the first Thursday after a show opens. The Sacramento Theatre Company also offers such a performance, but the date varies with each show.

STC also offers what it calls a "Hot Tix" deal. Come to the box office between noon and 1 P.M. on the day of the performance and you can buy a ticket at half price.

Miriam Gray's Acting Studio, which presents three or four performances a year, charges $12 for general admission. However, it also sells coupon books, each good for five admissions. Purchasers can use their coupons all at one show or spread them out over several productions. A coupon book costs $30, a 50-percent savings over single admissions. Many other theater companies accept coupons from discount travel, entertainment, and dining directories—typically, two admissions for the price of one.

And dinner theater? The *Bee* article points out that it is both a time and money saver. "Instead of going to a restaurant for dinner and then driving to a theater for a play, you can stay in one place and have both, often for less money." Garbeau's dinner theater, for example, charges $26 to $32 for both dinner and a show.

The article ran on the first page of one of the newspaper's Sunday sections, with a list of phone numbers for area theater companies on another page. Such an article in your own local paper is more than a benefit to the theaters—it's a service to the newspaper's readers. Point this out when you raise the idea with your local editor.

Audience Development

When sending out news releases, determine the recipients' reason to read your piece before writing anything, says Paul J. Krupin of Direct Contact Publishing. Then write a subject line that persuades your target to read your message. Remember your recipients are busy media professionals. There are two primary considerations on their mind: readership interest and editorial interest. Your title can make a difference between being read and possibly acted upon, or being tossed without being read.

Penmanship Counts

One PR person we know suggests you handwrite the address on the envelope. In this day and age of computer-generated mass mail, which envelopes do you open first? If you're like the majority of people, an envelope that is handwritten always is opened first. It's a simple but very effective way to gain an edge to get your name and information in front of the editor and, ultimately, in front of readers.

At Your Service

The Davis (California) Musical Theatre Company found good media coverage of its ticket giveaway to local charitable groups and area art directors. The company solicited applications from groups serving the local disadvantaged population and/or youth who have an interest in attending performances of the regular season or youth-theater productions. Requests for tickets were to be accompanied by "your group's name and a description of its charitable and/or educational purpose with regard to the disadvantaged and/or youth of our community. Also include your intended use of the tickets, the dates of three prioritized choices of shows you would like to attend, the number of tickets you would like," and a contact person.

Keeping Track

The Majestic Theatre Trust in Manchester, New Hampshire, sends out press releases to every newspaper (including school papers), radio station, and television station in its area for such things as auditions, ticket information, and fundraisers. Quite naturally, the company wants to know if the information it sends out is getting posted and published. Thus, an article in a recent edition of the Trust newsletter asks, "If you see a Majestic ad or info posted, clip it, save it, or let us know! We are interested in knowing who we are reaching and who on our lists are actually receiving and communicating the information." It's always a good idea to create an informal network like this to find out which publicity connections are working for you. Cultivate those while you work to find out how to make the others more productive as well.

First Impressions

The query letter is the most appropriate way to initiate contact with a newspaper, radio, or television station feature editor regarding a possible interview. The letter should be brief and work hard to sell the idea of an interview with the actor, director, board member, or whomever you are pushing. Don't talk about how important the interview is to your company; talk about how the interview will intrigue readers or listeners. Ideally, the person to be interviewed should be easy to talk to, with lots of good stories to relate. List briefly some of those stories to whet the editor's appetite. Finally, follow up with a phone call about a week later. If you've done a good job with the query letter, you'll find the editor much more receptive.

Lead from Strength

Want to get your news releases read—and used? Make your lead sentence as strong as possible. Here's one way: Focus on the most newsworthy point of the story and use it in the first sentence; reserve any other details for later. Try to reduce the essence of the news to a single sentence or even a single word. Here's one way to do it: Pretend you are calling a friend to report the news. You start with, "Do you know what happened?" "No," your friend replies, "what?" Your response to that question is your lead: "The board just voted to hire a volunteer coordinator."

Send a Card

Here's an idea that works for one publicity person. She looks for offbeat postcards that fit area media personalities and sends the pre-stamped card whenever she travels for personal or business reasons. "The response has been amazing and built stronger relationships, respect, and interaction," says Donna West of Yakima, Washington. "If the media hasn't received a card in a while, I'm asked why! They look forward to the cards!"

People Who Need People

Establish a "People" file for all the people you deal with on a regular basis. In each person's folder, place pertinent papers that reflect the working relationship you have with that person. Also include information on management styles, likes and dislikes, and other facts that will help you or others deal better with that person. This can be especially useful when asking for donations or other favors.

Got a Date?

Always include the days along with the dates when publicizing a production—for example, Friday, October 21. This approach will help prevent errors when your release or calendar item is used in a newspaper.

What's the Point?

For journalists, the first efforts to screen story ideas often involve rummaging through piles of letters, releases, and phone messages. If you want your idea to stand out, make it concise and with an obvious central idea that is easily grasped. Even better, present it in visual terms. Even print media people often grasp an idea better if they can visualize it.

Keeping Up-to-Date

Check your mailing list the next time you send out press releases or announcements. It doesn't make a good impression to mail to people who haven't been with a newspaper, say, for years. It's a good idea to call the media at least once a year and check to see if your names are still current.

A Single Voice

Choose one member of your company to be media spokesperson, and refer any questions from electronic or print media to that person. That way you can be certain you will have a consistent profile and that facts are given accurately. Obviously, your spokesperson should be chosen with care. You will need someone who knows the company well, understands the dynamics of your membership, and is accessible.

No News Is No News

We recently received a news release that began, "Though the title isn't known yet, you can be sure there will be plenty of theatrical events going on with the XXX Theatre throughout the month of October. Running every weekend in October, our main-stage show will be sure to contain something to please all. When we know exactly what the production is, we'll let you know immediately. But we'll be presenting theater every Thursday, Friday, and Saturday at 8 P.M., you can be sure." Most editors would toss this one immediately—probably while muttering unpleasantries at your theater company for wasting their time. To paraphrase Thumper the Rabbit, "If you can't say anything newsworthy about yourself, don't say anything at all." Otherwise, the next time you may find no one is paying any attention. Appropriately enough, this non-news release wasn't even dated.

Take Advantage of the "Photo Op"

Recently, a major metropolitan newspaper ran in its "metro" section three large photographs of children being made up by a makeup artist from a traveling performance company. "Seventh-grader Victor Bank discovers how opera can transform the ordinary into the extraordinary—or in this case, a male into a female," read the caption under the photograph. "Makeup specialist Sara Beukers, working with the Western Opera Theater, applies her wig techniques and makeup magic to Bank on Wednesday, who emerges as a gypsy woman from Verdi's *La Traviata*. The opera group, which is affiliated with the San Francisco Opera, gives in-school performances and seminars called 'Operatunities,' as well as community concerts in communities across the country." Did the newspaper photographer just happen to be at the school that day? Not likely. Is the three-photograph article evidence that a good photo opportunity shouldn't be wasted? Absolutely. Consider sending your own makeup or costume specialists to local schools, while informing print and electronic media that a good photo opportunity is there for the taking. Do this while you are in production, and the photo caption is likely to mention that as well.

No Strings

Never put conditions on any work you do with the media, especially, "If you put this press release in your paper and we get a good response, we'll consider advertising." If you want to pursue "hard" sales, call the advertising department. If you want to market your company and increase audience awareness, curry the favor of the editorial staff. Remember that the editorial and advertising departments are two different entities. Most honorable media outlets do not sell editorial coverage in return for advertising space. As a matter of fact, if you do offer this type of bribe, you will find your company will never get the editorial coverage it deserves. By working with the editorial staff and within the editorial guidelines of a publication, you can get the power of the press to work for your benefit.

Say Thanks

If a publication runs something about your company, whether it is a story, a press release, or whatever, send a thank-you note. Remember, a publication or radio station is giving you something free— something that costs them money, but assists you in getting the word out about your company. A thank-you will pay off large dividends in the future.

Brochures That Work

PART

III

A theater company's season brochure can be its single most important publicity tool. This is the one place where just about everything about your company is on display: its upcoming season, its choice of shows, its style, its quality. Many publicity people help in the development of the season brochure. If they don't, they *should*, or at least be in on the creative process, since the marketing points made in the brochure need to be repeated consistently throughout all publicity.

How to Design a Great Season Brochure | 12

If you're like most theater companies, your season brochure is your single most important marketing piece, followed by your general company brochure. Since so much rides on these pieces, it's important to understand exactly what works—and why.

Know Your Reader, Plan Every Inch, Keep It Simple

*L*et's start with two seemingly opposing principles. First, brochures often carry a lasting message. At least one study shows that half the people who receive a brochure will save it or pass it on to someone else. The more attractive and informative, the more likely the piece is to be saved. So it makes sense to plan and execute your season brochure with as much care as possible.

However, while the message may be lasting, the reader's attention is not. Again, studies indicate that when people pick up a brochure, most skim it, skipping around rather than reading from front to back. That makes writing brochures a challenge, because you can't assume the reader will read the information in the order it's placed on the page. Instead, each section of the brochure has to stand on its own to grab the reader's attention and provide necessary information.

There's no one right way to design a brochure. However, designers, printers, and direct-mail experts gave us three basic rules: Make it attractive, easy to read, and simple to follow.

Here are some suggestions gleaned from the same sources.

Text: *Short and Sweet*

There's no great secret to writing good brochures: Keep text short and to the point. Readers don't want to work hard to find what they need to know. So put yourself in the reader's place. What specific words are most likely to interest them? What kind of information are they likely to need? And what will they want to know first?

Write in personal terms so readers will feel you're talking to them. Use "you," "your," and "you're" whenever possible, as in "You'll experience a whole world of entertainment."

Avoid empty hyperbole when describing each show in the season. Don't say the show is wonderful and exciting—tell *why* the show is wonderful or exciting, as in "You'll gasp as the detective uncovers the murderer in the spine-tingling climax."

Be honest. Don't oversell your capabilities or set up false expectations.

Finally, when you write, keep in mind that short sections are easier to read. They also make the brochure design more inviting because you can break up the text with white space.

Envelope or Self-Mailer?

Most companies produce brochures that are mailed without envelopes. Such a "self-mailer" saves the cost of an envelope and may cut postage costs by reducing weight.

However, there is something to be said for the more personal look of an envelope addressed to the patron. So if you use an envelope, be sure to make it part of the sales package. If the envelope lacks interest, the brochure has to work that much harder. One simple solution is to buy envelopes with a distinctive color that also works with the brochure.

Whether you use an envelope or a self-mailer, the outside of the piece should use an illustration, theme, or line of copy from the brochure as a *teaser* (that is, a few words that compel the reader to open the piece). A teaser might read something like "America's favorite musical" or "You'll die laughing," followed by the words "See inside for more details" in smaller print.

As most direct-marketers point out, the most important thing is to get the reader to open your piece and have a look. Design the outside of your mailer with that in mind. If you go to the expense of using an envelope, don't defeat the purpose by using a mailing label; type or print directly on the envelope. Studies show a piece that looks individually addressed gets a better response.

Attention-Grabbing

The brochure's cover must grab the reader's attention. Use a strong photo or graphic that illustrates a single idea or concept. (See Part IV, beginning p. 65, for more about photos.) Keep words to a minimum and make the type big and easy to read. Like the design itself, the words should be simple, intriguing, and inviting.

Imagine you are passing out your brochure in some busy spot and it must attract attention as people stroll by. If your cover wouldn't grab *their* attention, it probably won't capture your intended audience's interest, either.

Format and Size

You may gain visibility if your brochure is different in shape and size from others that arrive in the mail. Study what your competitors are doing. Use a different format—one that helps you organize the information for your readers—or use a different way of folding.

One warning: The postal service will not accept just any size piece—nor will every standard envelope. Dimensions also affect the price; odd sizes can mean wastage when the printer trims the piece to size. Before spending money on a nonstandard-size piece, check with both your printer and the post office.

Design Considerations

Design is more than the way text and graphics are laid out on the page. Design also projects an image of your company and its season. You want to sell entertainment, fun, excitement, stimulation, and quality entertainment.

Be sure to consider the graphic sophistication of your reader. Arts patrons tend to be well educated and are accustomed to high-quality printing. If they're not familiar with your company, they may make a value judgment based on the quality (the writing, paper, photography, color) of your printed piece.

Color

Sure, it's expensive, but people are used to seeing color. And studies indicate that color does add to the effectiveness of a printed piece.

Two colors are fine, and you can use tints (*screens* in printer language) to vary the richness of the colors. For example, a 50-percent screen of red gives you pink. You also can overlap screens of two colors to give the impression of three colors: red and green overlapped become brown, yellow and blue become green, and so on.

Using Photos

Photographs give information quickly and memorably. Usually, a posed shot is better than one actually shot in performance, where focus and lighting can be troublesome. Come in close on the actors (preferably no more than three); keep distracting backgrounds to a minimum.

Avoid grouping several photographs into a collage; one strong photo is more likely to grab the reader. If you use more than one photo, make the strongest photo much larger than the others.

Put a caption on every photograph or other illustration; research shows that people look at a photo first, then the caption. Captions should sell, not merely describe.

When choosing photos, one designer suggests thinking how each photograph would work if your brochure were printed in a foreign language. In other words, ignore the words themselves and look at what the photo "says" about your company and its productions.

Other Art

Consider simple graphics or eye-catching illustrations to depict themes of plays. In fact, illustrations often work better than photos, because they often are simpler, with fewer elements, thus drawing more focus.

Testimonials

If you're still in the process of building community recognition, use testimonials—comments from critics or audience members. (If you aren't currently collecting testimonials, place a "Comment Box" in the lobby with a supply of 3 × 5 cards.)

Order Form

If the cover is the entry point to the brochure, the order form is the exit point. If the readers get this far, you know they are likely prospects. But it's here that many brochures are weakest.

The most common complaint about order forms is that they are too complicated. If you want good results, the form must be easy to understand. Keep details to the essentials. The design should lead the ticket-buyer through each step of the process so you collect all essential information. Another complaint is that order forms are too small, making it hard to write legibly. The best way to tell if your order form does its job well is to test it. Give copies to people who are unfamiliar with it and have them try to fill it out in your presence. Observe what they look for and how easily they find it. Be on the alert for signs of confusion, and listen to what they say.

Talk to your box-office or ticket-order people. Find out which mistakes purchasers make most often. Then review your order form to see if it can be improved to reduce these problems. Run all forms past the box-office manager to make sure the form is practical and contains all necessary information.

Review Results

When the subscription period ends, review the brochure and its impact. Keep what works, discard or improve what doesn't. Keep a file of brochures from other sources (theater-related or not) that have caught your attention, so you'll always have new ideas from which to draw.

Finally, think of your brochure as a theatrical production. Invest in it all the care and imagination that you would a play. Readers can and do make a connection between the quality of your printed piece and the quality of your productions.

13 | Brochures: Did You Know?

Type Casting

If you want your printed messages to come through loud and clear, avoid design techniques that hide the message. Among the worst offenders are these hard-to-read blunders: red type on a pink background; type superimposed on colorful artistic backgrounds; italic type used extensively on a gray background; long text blocks set in reverse type (white on black); and almost anything printed on dark-colored or aggressively fluorescent paper. The latter may work well for posters that have few words set in large-point type, but it can cause headaches for readers when used for brochures or flyers.

Plan Ahead

When you design brochures and other pieces, you can save money by planning ahead. For example, design your art so you can use it more than once—on a brochure or in a newspaper ad. If you know that you'll be mailing large quantities of the same brochure or similarly sized brochures, but not all at once, you can preprint some components in large quantities (such as response envelopes) and save money. And if a piece isn't date-sensitive (such as a general company brochure or a yearlong campaign), don't put a date on it. That way, you can use it over a longer period.

Getting Help

An idea from the newsletter of the Oklahoma Community Theatre Association: Approach a local advertising agency to design a season-ticket brochure for nothing. Such a project gives the agency the chance to be innovative and creative, as well as something it can enter in a design contest, and you get a great mailer. Just be sure to agree in advance that any design they come up with can be produced at a reasonable cost.

Keep It Simple

With the proliferation of desktop publishing, more and more novices are overdoing the use of the many typefaces (known as fonts) available. By mixing a large number of fonts on the same page of a newsletter, ad, or brochure, people tend to create an ugly jumble of type. Doubts? Look at an excellent ad or newsletter. How many different typefaces to do see? Most likely there won't be many. Clean up your act and you may find yourself cleaning up in ticket sales as well.

Fair Trade Plan

Offer to include your printing company's name on your high-profile printed pieces (such as mailers, brochures, and programs) in exchange for a reduced price. You save on your most impressive pieces and the printer gets a free testimonial advertisement.

Weighing In

Use an electronic postage scale to count large numbers of identical booklets or brochures. Stack them on the scale until you reach one pound; then count the number. The simple math involved in weighing a few brochures and then multiplying can save lots of time over counting individual pieces by hand.

Color Blind?

Be careful about colors in a brochure. We recently saw an expensive brochure with six large photographs printed in dark green with text overprinted in dark purple. The result was unreadable. In some cases the text could have been reversed out—that is, printed as white letters on the dark background. But some of the photographs had light areas on which the reversed-out text would have been invisible. When faced with such a problem, decide which is more important— the photograph or the text. If it's the text, then have the printer screen the photographs to 30 to 40 percent of their original darkness. They still will be visible, but won't compete with the text. If the photograph is more important, don't run text over it. Use text beside or below, or in a box inset into the photo.

Overdo It

Print more than you need of brochures and flyers. It's easier and less expensive to toss out old material than to put a job back on the press for reprints. The cost for additional copies usually isn't significant when compared to the total cost of a job.

Taking Stock

If possible, use the same paper stock for more than one publication or flyer. You might be able to get a quantity discount.

Adding Color

Want to turn a two-color print job into a three-color one without the added cost? Prepare your camera-ready copy for two colors, but change one of the colors when the sheet is printed on the reverse side. For example, use black and red on one side and black and blue on the other. The publication will appear to be printed in three colors, but your cost should be the same as with a two-color press run, with only a small charge for washing the press between runs of the two sides.

Here's Proof

When a proof of a brochure or flyer must be circulated to and approved by several people, don't circulate the same copy to each person in turn. This may result in people trying to "outdo" each other by finding "mistakes" and making suggestions. Instead, give them each their own copy and tell them you will coordinate their comments. You'll get fewer unnecessary changes. It's faster, too.

Color Issues

Check with your quick-print shop to see if they offer special prices for certain colors on certain days. It's easier for a printer to run several jobs once a color is set up (presses have to be washed down when a color is changed). If your print shop doesn't offer discounts on particular days, ask if you can get a price break by scheduling your job with a similar one to avoid the extra cost of press setup.

Cutting Paper Costs

Here's a way to find less expensive but high-quality papers for brochures, flyers, and programs. Ask your printers for swatchbooks of their house stocks. These are papers of equivalent quality to brand-name papers, but far less expensive. You'll save ordering time as well.

Avoiding Clutter

When producing a brochure, avoid using many small photographs, which detract from rather than enhance visual communication. Ideally, use one strong photograph. If you have two or more photographs, make sure one is dominant. Square photographs lack visual interest; use other rectangular shapes with a mixture of horizontal and vertical orientation.

More on Color

Instead of printing a brochure on colored paper, ask your printer how much it would cost to print on the "house brand" of white paper of equivalent quality, on which he screens a second color to approximate the color of paper you want. For example, a 10-percent screen of a dark blue will give a light-blue color to the paper. In many cases, the cost for screening may be significantly less than with colored paper. An additional advantage: You can use the same second color unscreened (that is, at 100 percent) to emphasize a headline or graphic element.

Print Scheduling

Plan to have materials printed at times when printers are less busy. For example, avoid school openings, the beginning of a new year, and major holidays. Reason: You can expect to receive lower bids when printers aren't busy.

Photographs

Theater is about words and images. In your publicity mix, you'll want to provide potential audience members with strong visuals that help them understand what your production and your theater are about, as well as underscoring the high quality of that production and of your company.

Catching an Editor's Eye

Advice on How to Make Sure Your Photos Wind Up Getting Printed

NEIL OFFEN

14

As an editor, I receive a bundle of press releases almost every day. I must confess that I don't read most of them. I simply don't have the time. Some I don't even look at, knowing instantly that the subject is not of interest to me. With others, I'll read the first paragraph or two, seeing if anything grabs my attention.

The only exception to my habit is a press release with photographs. No matter what the envelope says, or the first paragraph indicates, if the press release has a photograph enclosed with it, I'll take a look. That's because, like all editors, I'm always on the lookout for items that will make my publication more graphically interesting, and nothing does that better than photographs.

Any press release that comes with photos has an immediate advantage with me, but if the photo is not good, that advantage is quickly squandered. Too often, I can see that I just will not be able to use the picture. Why? Here are some of the reasons and what to avoid when you send in photos with your releases.

1. *It's not sharp.* This may seem basic, but all publications want to use only sharp, well-focused shots. If your publicity

shot is blurred, if the people in the shot are fuzzy, not only will editors not use the photo, but you also will be creating a negative image of your company as amateurish and lacking in quality. If there's no one in your company on whom you can rely to take sharp, well-focused photographs, then hire an outside photographer or trade services with one.

2. *There are too many people in the picture.* Most newspapers—and even some magazines—don't run photographs very large, particularly if the shots are not part of a big feature or news story. Consequently, if there are too many people in the photo—if it's a shot, say, of a big ensemble scene—it's likely everybody in the photo will be much too small in the reproduction. There will be nothing to focus the reader's eye on, and no one or nothing will be easily identifiable.

3. *The people in the photo aren't doing anything.* The reason editors want photos is that they make the page more visually interesting. But if the people in the picture are just standing there, or looking straight out at the camera, that goal isn't achieved. So have the people in the photo do something engaging. Let them wear interesting costumes or use interesting props. For example, if you're promoting an upcoming Shakespearean production, let your actors strike a fencing pose, arms up and outstretched. Even if your Shakespearean costumes aren't ready yet, the poses can suggest them.

4. *No caption is included.* Pictures frequently come into my office without any identification at all. Not the name of the company, not the play, not the people in the shot. Perhaps some of that information can be found in the accompanying release. But with all the releases coming in to an editor, hunting for caption information is too much extra work. The release may get separated from the photos, or may go to a different editor. It doesn't matter how visually interesting a picture is if there is no information on who the people are and what, exactly, they are doing. Make sure the captions are attached to or written directly on the back of the photo with a nonsmear marker. The caption information always should include the name of the play, the name of the theater company, the name(s) of the actors, the dates of the show, and the name and address of the theater.

5. *The deadline is passed.* Make sure your photos are on time. If your production is opening on Saturday, don't send photos out to the newspaper two days before. Newspapers have deadlines, particularly for items that are not "breaking news." Newspaper

weekend supplement sections, for instance, frequently are completed almost a week ahead of their actual cover date. Make sure your photos get to editors a long time in advance. If you're not sure of the deadlines for a particular media outlet, call and find out.

6. *There's no choice.* As long as you're sending photos, why not send more than one? Give the editor a choice. Make one vertically oriented and another horizontally oriented. That way, if the editor has a particular hole on a page that he needs to fill (which often can happen at the last moment), you can fill the bill. You also might send a shot with just one or two actors in it, and another with a somewhat larger group. Again, this gives the editor different options.

7. *The people in the photo don't look very good.* All the actors in your photographs should be looking their best. Editors, just like audiences, can be turned off by looking at people who don't seem to care about their appearance. Make sure your actors look just as good as they would onstage.

8. *It's the wrong kind of photo.* If the newspaper doesn't use color photographs, why send in color photos? If they only use slides, why send in prints? Call up the media outlet and ask what kind of format is needed. You shouldn't waste your time—or your company's money.

15 | *Worth a Thousand Words*

Underscoring the Need for Good Photos

STEPHEN PEITHMAN

I know that Neil Offen's tips on publicity photos in Chapter 14 really work, because my experience as a publicist has taught me the same lessons.

I make a point of making sure the photographs are just of one, two, or three people. The only time I break this rule is when I know the photo will be used large, as on the cover of a weekend arts supplement.

We shoot everything at the photographer's studio. At one time, we shot at the theater or rehearsal space, but the studio has better (that is, less distracting) backdrops, and lighting can be controlled exactly. I use a husband-and-wife team of professional photographers who give us a discount because we mention their studio in the program. (They also take part of their payment in tickets.)

I refuse to shoot publicity photos outside in actual settings, like parks or on the steps of old houses. People will be seeing a play, not a film, and I feel that publicity photos should be *theatrical*.

In many cases, the costumes in the photos are the ones used in the show, but we often pull from stock pieces if the actual costumes aren't done yet. As soon as the show begins rehearsal, I work with the costume designer on the shoot to make sure we have what we need.

Directing a photo shoot is a little like directing a play. Do all you can to make the actors comfortable. I keep the sessions brisk, make jokes, get them to relax. I also bring props; one silk rose of mine has been in at least six publicity shoots; so has a set of champagne glasses. Props give actors something to do and often make them feel more at ease in front of the camera.

I make sure characters are totally focused on one another. When I break the rule, it's for a reason—to show the alienated heroine looking away from her would-be lover, for example, or the cast of *Pinafore* singing their hearts out directly to the viewer. I aim for the best pose, even if it doesn't actually occur onstage. However, the photo must never show something the characters would not do; it should always reflect the spirit of the play.

The value of good photographs is easily seen. The ones I've taken have done multiple duty in ads, brochures, and newsletters.

16 | Photographs: Did You Know?

Who's That?

When sending publicity photos to a newspaper, make sure each is captioned and labeled. Type the caption onto a piece of plain white paper, including the name of your theater company, the name of the show, production dates, the names of the people in the shot, and the name of the person who took the photograph. (The paper used for this should be smaller than the size of the photograph itself.) Tape the paper to the back of the photograph. Never write directly on a photograph; the ink may smear and the point of a ballpoint pen or pencil will go through the paper and damage the picture.

Details Count

A publicity photograph in a local newspaper showed the cast of *Arsenic and Old Lace*. While some care had been exercised in getting the leads into appropriate costume, the bad-fitting wig for one of the Brewster sisters gave a slipshod look to the photo. Think about it: How would *you* judge the quality of the show when there is a half-inch gap between a wig and the actor's forehead? Audiences make quick judgments based on whatever evidence is before them. You don't have much time to make an impression. Even the smallest details can win—or lose—a potential audience member.

Ups and Downs

When you prepare publicity photos, compose the photos vertically. Editors with limited newspaper space tend to choose such photos to fit their one-column spots.

Not Pretty As a Picture

We recently came across a color publicity photograph that at first glance appeared to be taken in a wax museum. The cause seemed to be heavy makeup and the result was somewhat repellent, particularly with a young man who had all the animation of a department store mannequin. To avoid the problem, instruct your actors to use makeup sparingly. Remember that a camera is like an audience member sitting three or four feet away.

Posters and Ads

*M*any forms of publicity provide you with little or no control over the finished product. When you submit a release, for example, the editor can change or cut words at will. If you want your message to look and read exactly as you created it, you need to produce the finished product yourself for use as a poster or advertisement. Here are some thoughts on both methods.

Posters: Are They Worth the Trouble?

Sometimes—But You Need to Know When

*P*osters are among the most popular forms of publicity in theater—and sometimes the least effective.

Successful publicity means: (1) getting a message to those people who most likely will be interested in hearing it; (2) putting the message in a form that makes it easy for them to receive it; (3) presenting the message at a time in which they are most likely to pay attention to it; and (4) providing a message that will create a positive response.

Posters often score poorly in these departments. First, they are the most general of publicity tools. They usually are put up in store windows, on bulletin boards, or in any free space that can be found. The problem is, of course, that even if they are noticed, there's no guarantee *playgoers* will see them. Thus, when putting up posters, think of places where theatergoers are likely to congregate—near movie theaters, for example, or restaurants, church bulletin boards, faculty lounges. Try to place your poster by itself, away from others, or where only one or two posters can fit. Posters work best when they are alone, or very large, or have some other way of attracting attention or standing out from the environment.

Second, consider the mental state of people who pass by your poster. They are most likely not out looking at walls, windows, or bulletin boards. They have things on their minds, errands to run, tasks to accomplish. If they see your poster at all, it may be only for a fleeting second. If they do stop to look, they may not have enough time to read more than a few words or be able to remember the entire message. They may not have anything to write with in order to capture the information. If a poster is to work at all in such an environment, it needs to be brief and to the point. (More on that in a moment.)

Third, passersby are not the best audience for posters. People are more likely to read one if they see it while standing in one place for a minute or so. Therefore, good locations include waiting areas in restaurants and medical offices, as well as lounges, lunchrooms, lobbies, foyers, meeting rooms, and laundromats.

Fourth, the message should be simple and direct. Too many posters give more information than necessary. Studies show people respond best to small chunks of information, in large type, and worded in such a way that a response is fairly simple. (Think of a billboard you might see along a highway.) At most, your poster should contain the name of the show, the playwright, show dates, the theater location, and where to get ticket information. Omit ticket prices and names other than the author of the play (unless specified by the contract). Make sure the ticket-sales location and phone number is printed large. At the very least, if a person can walk away with nothing more than the name of the play and your theater company, he or she should be able to look up your number in the phone book.

In general, posters should be seen as a support tool in your publicity campaign. If you are spending a lot of money on them, don't. Most groups find that a good-quality photocopied poster on heavy paper will do as well as something printed by a professional printer, at least in quantities under a thousand.

Posters should be on white or a light-color paper. Avoid dark colors because they don't allow enough contrast for lettering to be visible from 10 feet away. When designing a poster, try several color combinations, print them out on a color printer, and tack them together on a wall. From 10 feet, which reads best? Avoid fluorescent (Day-Glo) paper except for yellow or perhaps orange. While these certainly do get attention, their very brightness makes reading the text difficult. If you must use a bright color, keep text large (24-point type or higher). The darker or brighter the color, the larger the type necessary for readability.

Although direct-mail, newspaper, radio, and television publicity is more effective, posters do have a place. They reinforce the other publicity, for one thing. They also catch a few people who might not see or hear the other publicity. They also generate team spirit by getting the cast and crew involved in putting up posters in the community or surrounding town. (Always print enough extra posters for cast and crew to keep as souvenirs.)

Have some method to track where posters will go, a list of locations for which people can sign up. There also should be a check to see that posters are still up; many get ripped down or covered with other posters. A list also helps make sure posters are removed after the show is over.

To sum up: Use posters, but don't base your entire publicity campaign on them. They are just one tool in your effort to spread the word.

A Special Case

There is one way posters can be made more effective. Audiences love to see familiar faces on stage—and it doesn't have to be a Broadway star, either. It might be a friend or coworker.

You can capitalize on this—and boost ticket sales in the process—by producing mini-posters that feature photos of individual performers and then posting them in the offices or organizations where they work.

Use a computer-layout program such as PageMaker to create a template for a standard 8½ × 11-inch sheet of paper. The basic design is the same for each poster, with the name of the show, dates, and ticket information. In the center of the poster, draw a box the size of the photographs you plan to use. (All photos will need to be the same size and shape.)

Individualize each poster by adding the name of the employee/performer. (If you use PageMaker, put the repeated information on the master page and the individual names on the regular pages.) Mention the role the person will play, especially if it's not a lead.

Print the posters, then glue on the color photo of the employee. If the company is a large one and you need more than one or two posters, make color photocopies that include the photograph.

This kind of publicity does double duty. Besides advertising your show and encouraging ticket sales, it's a morale booster for the performers. It gives them something to be proud of and shows your theater company cares about them as well.

18 | Sell Sizzle, Not Steak

When Writing Ads, Make Every Word Count

*T*he problem with most nonprofessionally produced theater ads is that they don't *sell*—they merely announce. Their message is, "We're having a play on these dates." How well do you think Pepsi would sell if its ads said only, "We've got this cola"? There are other colas, after all, and there are other things people can be doing besides going to your play. In other words, people make choices, and your ad should help them choose *you*.

To create a good ad, don't begin with what you want to promote. Instead, concentrate on your target audiences, their needs and concerns. The average person is exposed to hundreds of advertising messages every day and screens out most of them. The ones that get through are those that address his or her concerns or interests.

It's the benefit, more often than not, that the customer is actually buying, whether they know it or not. That's why Eastman Kodak sells memories in its consumer advertising before it sells film. It's why automobile manufacturers promise prestige, excitement, image, even the personality and style with which buyers wish to associate. It's all summed up in the old advertising cliche, "Sell the sizzle, not the steak."

Of course, you must provide basic information: show name, dates, times, perhaps prices. But consider these two points as well: (1) only a small percentage of those who read a newspaper or watch television are a potential theater audience, and (2) of these, only a small number will attend based on the play title alone.

In other words, while a newspaper may have thousands of readers, only a relative handful will be reached by your ad. This does not mean you shouldn't advertise—it means you must make your ad as powerful as you can.

To Each Its Own

Each production needs its own advertising style. If the show is well known, trade on that: "the Broadway hit." If it's not well known, entice the reader with a promise of entertainment: "the murder mystery classic" or "the uproarious comedy." Other phrases can help build audiences: "an adult comedy" or "a treat for the entire family." Take a look at each show and jot down what you think are its most saleable points. (This means you must know the play well; don't sell what isn't there.) Then use your strongest selling point only.

Ad Placement

Where should you place your ad? A large metropolitan daily has a huge readership, but its costs are also high because ad rates are based on *total* readers, not on the number who may be potential theatergoers. Many metropolitan areas have weekly papers that feature entertainment news. Their rates are much lower, and you may find they reach your potential audiences as well or better than the big papers.

The best way to measure which papers work for you is to devise a response mechanism. A classic one is "Mention this ad and get $1 off each ticket." Place this ad in one paper only in order to count the number of people pulled in by your ad. Try the dollar-off ad in various publications and compare the results. Base your future ad purchases on these results and the cost of the ad. An ad in a daily newspaper may pull a good response, but the cost of the ad may eat up the gains.

Some companies routinely ask ticket-buyers, "How did you find out about our production?" The problem here is that they may say, "A friend told me," and you have no way of knowing whether the friend saw your ad or heard about your show from some other source.

Another approach is to place an ad in the program of another theater production. The cost certainly will be less than an ad in a daily newspaper, and you can be assured that everyone who reads the ad is a potential patron for your own production. If the other company doesn't have advertising in its program, ask whether they will take an insert—a separate sheet of the same dimensions as the program, but totally produced by you. Since you are providing the insert, you should not be charged as much as for an ad.

Summing Up

Advertising should be just one part of your total marketing effort, not the whole ball game. Advertising can't enable your company to overcome a bad artistic decision. Even the best advertising can't improve a poorly directed show or one for which there is no market. In fact, good advertising can make a poor production fail faster by bringing in more people who try it, reject it, and then tell others. This, in turn, may hurt audiences for future productions.

A good ad considers both the information you want to get across (dates, times, place) and the information the reader needs to make a decision (Will I enjoy it?).

Creating More Effective Ads | 19

S urprise: Sometimes the name of your show is not the lead for your ad. Unless the show is well known to most of the ad's readers, the response to the title of the play may well be, "So what?"

The best ads begin with a headline that offers a benefit or proposition that will attract and interest your target audience. The headline should usually be emphasized in bold type, larger than your body copy and logo.

Let's say you are doing a play such as *A Comedy of Errors*. Is Shakespeare going to sell the show? Is the title? The answer depends on your audience. It may be that you must begin with something like: "laugh your socks off" or "an evening of riotous laughter" or something similar. If it is a recent play that has had a New York run, quote something from one of the New York papers. Many large libraries have copies of the New York Drama Critics annuals, which reproduce all reviews of New York openings; if yours doesn't, ask about an interlibrary loan.

A photo or illustration is a big help. Photos are the most troublesome, because they are so precisely a representation of reality. If the photo does not accurately convey the mood of the piece, it will not attract. For example, if you are doing a fantasy and the photo clearly shows heavy stage makeup or poorly constructed costumes, what does that do for the fantasy? Better to use an illustration. If you don't have an artist in your company, check royalty-free sources, like Dover Books' collections. Much good clip art is available for computer use—just make sure it is of high quality. In any case, the simpler and bolder the art, the more effective it will be.

Do You Know the 75/25 Rule?

20

In Ads, Percentages Count

*I*f you take time to glance through magazine advertisements, you'll find that most adhere to a simple design rule: Use 75 percent of the space for a graphic and headline, and only 25 percent for specific information. (In some cases, professionals go even higher, with 80 percent or more for the graphic.)

The idea is that the graphic and headline draw the reader's attention and lead into the 25 percent that is the sales message. There must be something to this design concept because it is, by far, the most common in professionally designed ads. In contrast, think of how many theatrical ads or posters you may have seen that seem to shoehorn in as much information as possible, with no single element to catch the eye or sell the show in question.

We've created two ads (they could just as easily be posters) using the 75/25 rule, shown in the illustration on page 84. The ad at the left is dominated by a graphic that makes clear the subject of the play. In part, this is because the title isn't a familiar one, and the drawing of the mouse explains it quickly. In case there is any doubt, the title is followed by "A musical play for children." All this so far is part of

the 75 percent because the three elements—drawing, title, and explanation—are directly connected. The 25 percent at the bottom is the specific information on dates, place, and ticket information.

The ad on the right is slightly different. Here, the graphic supports the more important large-type copy: "You'll laugh. You'll cry. You'll save." Together they make up the 75 percent. The remainder is the list of the season's plays and season-ticket information. Take a look at your own ads and posters and see if you can improve their readability by applying the 75/25 rule. Remember that people are often in a hurry. They scan a page or a wall quickly. Your message needs to be simple and direct—and part of a total design that catches the eye.

Absolutely Free!

The best way to get a good response from an ad is to announce a free offer in your headline. (The headline for this paragraph caught your attention, didn't it?) This shouts to readers that they can get something without charge. What you offer doesn't have to be expensive. For example, you might offer a pen with your theater logo on it, a calendar, or some other inexpensive item. Or offer a free ticket for every three purchased for a weeknight performance.

Look for the Silver Liner

Although this idea comes from a Texas community college, it is easily adapted to a theater company. A few years ago, San Jacinto College in Pasadena, Texas, approached several fast-food restaurants and public-school food services in the area about supplying them with paper tray liners that tout programs at the college. This year's tray-liner design utilizes interactive crossword puzzles, multiple-choice quizzes, jumbles, word searches, and other brainteasers to get across various messages about the college as people eat. The college prints several hundred thousand tray liners for use throughout the spring and summer months. Restaurants such as McDonald's and Burger King accept them readily.

Other Issues

Publicity covers such a wide spectrum of tools that many don't fit into neat, tidy categories. When we asked *Stage Directions* readers, "What's the Best Publicity Tool Your Company Uses?," we heard a variety of answers that prove how wide that spectrum really is.

For example, James Carver, formerly of Kalamazoo Civic Theatre in Michigan, advised that "an attractive mass mailer will pull in people who otherwise might not attend your show. It's well worth the time and money spent, especially if it truly reflects the spirit of your production."

Alan Harvey, of San Francisco's Lamplighters, said his company also relies on direct mail. "We often share mailing lists with similar groups. Sometimes we share partial lists, since the computer is capable of culling names to our specifications. We remove those who have not bought tickets for two years. Our normal list has 6,000 names."

Ed Henry, of Theater Cleveland, had a different take. "Good reviews are the best publicity and they're free," he said. "Beyond that, I think direct mail works best. There's lots of competition out there. As a PR idea, try to get some local critics involved in some of your company's decision making.

When they see their own ideas brought to life onstage, they will think you are wonderful. Besides, many of them are pretty knowledgeable and have much to contribute."

A more philosophic approach was taken by Charlene Baldridge, of Old Globe Theatre in San Diego. "No matter what idea you might have," she said, "the answer is in the name. Neil Simon always sells out. Also, all the public relations campaigns in the world won't work unless you work on your internal image. Then the quality will show. Remember not to try getting the attention of the critics before you're ready, and be careful about the accuracy of the information in your program."

Following are some other ideas from the pages of *Stage Directions*.

Cyberspace Promotion | *22*

As no one needs to be reminded, the media have changed greatly in the last few years. Cable and satellite television has splintered the viewing audience. Deregulation in radio has caused the replacement of local small-town stations with far-away satellite-downloaded programming. And, of course, the computer revolution has fundamentally changed not just the way people work, but also the way we receive—and, for that matter, contribute—information. While newspaper circulation continues to diminish, more and more people now get their news from the Internet and the World Wide Web.

How can you take advantage of the Internet to publicize your show and your theater? Here are some ideas.

How to Push Your Theater on the Information Superhighway

Scott Miller

*I*f you're trying to publicize your show, nothing can take the place of good old-fashioned news releases, public service announcements, and schmoozing with the press. However, the emerging information superhighway does offer a number of new possibilities to promote your productions in your area.

When my company, New Line Theatre, presented the world premiere of a new musical, *In the Blood*, we began with a public reading and discussion of the show. I used my home computer, the America Online service, and the Internet to promote the reading and the show. (The methods I used also would work with Prodigy, CompuServe, and any other on-line services with Internet connections.)

America Online offers two sites for people to post messages about musical theater—*Saturday Review Online* and *The New York Times Online*. Both have theater boards and dozens of folders on topics ranging from Sondheim and Lloyd Webber to tech theater to ideas for auditions. America Online has strict rules about "selling" anything on the public boards. Still, I could post a variation of my press release, talking about the show and the dates, and telling people to e-mail me if they wanted more information, as long as I didn't mention ticket prices. (It's acceptable, however, to "sell" through private e-mail and mention ticket prices.)

On the Internet through the Usenet (user's network), you can access discussion groups, called *news groups*, on hundreds of different theater topics, including musical theater.

Because the Internet isn't controlled by any one company or organization, rules are almost nonexistent, and I could be much more upfront there about selling tickets. I now had access to thousands of people around the world. News of our world premiere musical reached more people than I could have dreamed of, and all of them could e-mail me for more info if they wanted—and all at no cost to our company.

E-Mail to the Rescue

But there's more. Recently, I began to e-mail copies of my news releases to all my friends on-line without spending money on printing or postage. I also discovered that I could ask the America Online system to search member records and give me a list of everybody with the words *musical* and *theater* in their member profile. Or if I wanted to reach only local people, I could ask it to search for people with *musical*, *theater*, and *St. Louis* (or *Missouri*) in their profiles.

Through this search, I had a ready-made mailing list of local musical-theater enthusiasts; using the e-mail address-book feature, I stored a "St. Louis Musical Theater" mailing list in my computer. Now when I want to send an e-mail press release, I just click on that list and my one piece of e-mail is automatically sent to a hundred people simultaneously.

Since the show I was promoting, *In the Blood*, is about a vampire and a hematologist who fall in love, I also used America Online to search for people listing vampires among their interests. Presto—yet another mailing list for a special vampire-related news release.

But I wasn't done yet. When I receive e-mail from someone, it's possible to forward a copy of that mail to someone else with a note attached from me. This opened up another possibility. A friend on-line who is a gay activist has compiled an extensive electronic mailing list of his own. Because *In the Blood* also involved gay themes, I e-mailed my activist friend a press release emphasizing the show's gay angle, and asked him to forward it to his own mailing list. He was able to take my e-mail and forward it to dozens more people. Other friends with different lists did the same. Soon, I had created a pyramid PR mailing. I could e-mail one person, who then would forward my press release to many more people—who could forward it to their friends, and so on.

Cheaper by the Thousands

By the time I was done, I had reached thousands of people with information about *In the Blood* who were specifically targeted because of their interests. I also discovered several local newspapers, television news departments, feature writers, and critics who were on-line, so I could contact them easily about doing feature stories.

There isn't a more powerful way to market your show because you're getting information out to people who already have shown some interest in what you do. (Despite your research, some of those who receive your e-mail will not be pleased; if someone requests to be removed from your list, do so promptly and let them know you have done so.)

The only cost of all this was my time on-line, and because I wrote my news release off-line and then signed on just to send it, my on-line time was minimal. Total cost for all my public relations efforts was about $5. To reach so many people with traditional printed material would have cost my company thousands of dollars.

None of these high-tech methods will replace mailing news releases, PSAs, or promotional flyers—at least not for the near future. But as a supplement to tried-and-true publicity methods, the information superhighway opens up the possibility of reaching thousands of people instantly.

23 | First Get Their Attention

Why Publicity Stunts Have Their Place

WYCLIFFE MCCRACKEN

*P*ublicity stunts are a time-honored tradition in theater, and still can be a useful tool to spark ticket sales.

While preparing for a production of *Annie Get Your Gun* (based on the life of sharpshooter Annie Oakley), I suddenly wondered if there might be any families named Oakley in the area. The phone book indicated that three families by that name lived in the vicinity. Voila! I contacted two of my horse-loving students, clothed them in Western garb, and let the newspapers know that free tickets (once known in the trade as "Annie Oakleys") would be delivered to these modern-day Oakleys' front door via "cowpunchers" on horseback. The way the news spread was exciting—and so were ticket sales.

The Oakley connection is a good example of a tie-in—linking your production with someone or something in your community. Such a link may well create news, and thus a mention (or more) in your local media.

For example, when we did the musical *High Button Shoes*, we publicized the fact that this was the same area where it was originally scripted. When we produced *War of the Worlds*, we used a caravan of cars to carry a wreath of flowers to the exact spot in New Jersey where the "invasion from Mars" was supposed to have occurred. The newspapers covered our "memorial service" very nicely.

If you can't find an obvious connection, create one. For example, many communities have a program in which a high school student becomes "Mayor" or "Superintendent of Schools" or "Chief of Police" for a day. When something like this occurred in our city, I persuaded the high school "chief" to arrange his "cops" in a semicircle around blown-up pictures of the villains in our mystery play. The caption above the pictures was, naturally, a large "WHODUNIT?" Tread carefully, however. For one play, I released helium balloons with tickets attached. One farmer brought in a ticket he had secured via a careful rifle shot. Obviously, this type of advertising gimmick might cause problems.

One of the best publicity ideas I've used wasn't a stunt at all. A stack of stamped cards, a table, pens, and a phone book with addresses was a regular part of rehearsals. Cast and crew reminded friends and family of the upcoming production—and a surprising number responded.

24 | What's in a Name? Maybe an Audience

Local Personalities Make for Good Promotion

*I*f it works within the framework of a production, you can get considerable publicity mileage by casting a well-known local personality in your show, perhaps in a walk-on or small role suited to their talent (if any). We know of several companies who have done this to good effect.

One company used "guest stars" from the community in small or walk-on roles in several of its productions. The guest actors (variously, members of the city council, the mayor, a county supervisor) were announced in press releases, and the celebrities' friends and families helped fill the house—as did a certain number of curiosity-seekers. Surprisingly, there were few ego problems—most of the celebrities were flattered to be asked to perform and accepted direction easily. While we can't say their performances rated raves, their involvement probably had a great deal to do with their later support for the theater's request for a city subsidy.

A midsized opera company used local celebrities to lip-synch arias from well-known operas, including county supervisors, city council members, and radio and television personalities. Judges included the city's mayor, as well as the opera company's general director and conductor. A theater group might do the same with songs from musical comedies.

If you've already turned craven coward at the thought of non-actors on stage, you might follow the lead of another group, which asks local celebrities to act as hosts, taking tickets at the door and welcoming theatergoers. Each host has a name tag so there is no doubt as to who the host is.

Using celebrity hosts not only adds prestige to the event, but also again links the movers and shakers of your community with your company. (By the way, the hosts get free seats to the performance for which they host.)

Finally, we present what seems to us a died-and-gone-to-heaven situation. In one city, the two most popular radio morning-show hosts also participate in community-theater productions. Hardly a week goes by without one of them mentioning a play they are in or are directing, or a play by one of the companies for which they act. If you're out scouting for potential actors, you might give some thought to which of your local media personalities could benefit your company onstage and off.

25 | Getting Them There
A Good Map Will Do the Trick

After looking at several maps included in theater promotional material, it seems to us that many theater companies need help to do better. In almost every case we noted, the maps included were too small, too complex, or too vague.

Is a map necessary? If your theater is located on a main thoroughfare, is well lighted, and visible from the street, probably not. If the theater is none of the above, you need to consider how to make your map easily readable.

First of all, a good map is oriented so north is at the top of the drawing. Follow this convention so you don't confuse readers.

Second, reduce information to a minimum. For example, you don't need to show every street that crosses the one on which your theater is located—just the nearby ones and perhaps one or two other main streets. If your patrons will need to exit from a freeway, indicate the *exact* name of the exit and which direction to take once they leave the freeway.

Third, take a look at maps that automobile dealers use in their newspaper ads. These maps are often excellent models on which to base your own map. You'll note that they follow all of these rules.

The map shown here is based on the most complex situation—guiding patrons through a major metropolitan area. Note that the downtown area is merely indicated, and that only main streets and freeway exits are shown. The entrance to the theater's parking lot is clearly defined. This is about the right size for a map. Any smaller and some people will have a hard time reading it (particularly in a car); any larger and it will take up too much room in a brochure or ticket envelope.

This map was drawn using a computer graphics program. However, hand-drawn maps can be effective too. The trick is to draw the map at least twice the actual print size, using a fine-tip black pen (avoid other colors or ballpoint pens). Don't hand-letter unless you're a calligrapher; it's better to type or use a computer printer to produce the street names, then cut them out and paste them on the map. Because the original map is twice its eventual size, you'll find it easier to paste on the words. When you're done, reduce the map to 50 percent of its original size on a high-quality copy machine. Then use that copy to paste on the camera-ready copy of your brochure or flyer before printing.

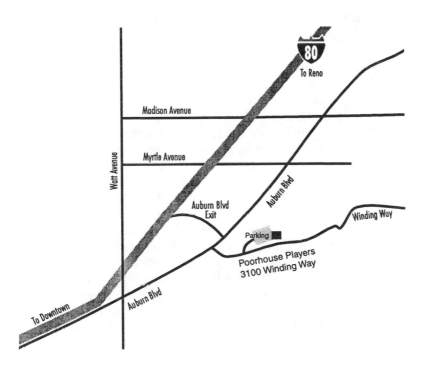

26 | Working with Reviewers

How to Get Them on Your Side—and What to Do When Things Go Wrong

Reviewers: Can't live with them, can't live without them. We get angry when we aren't reviewed, and angry when we read anything negative about our production, because we know that many people wait for the reviews to decide whether to attend a show.

Getting reviewers to see a show usually is the responsibility of the publicity person. The best way to handle reviews is the same way you handle the media in general—build rapport with your local arts editor and reviewers. Keep them informed about your company and its artistic development, and give them enough advance notice so they can schedule a review for opening night. In metropolitan areas, reviewers may have many different productions to cover, so the sooner you can get on the schedule, the better.

Once you have established a rapport with a reviewer, work directly with the person, if possible. Send him or her copies of all your press releases and a personal invitation to review. It is still the editor's job to assign a reviewer, but if a critic says, "I'd like to review the Poorhouse Players production next week," he or she probably will get the go-ahead.

Always have a packet of information for the reviewers

when they pick up their tickets at the box office. This should include a copy of the program, a fact sheet about the production (including production dates, times, and ticket prices), and, if possible, some background about the show. The latter is especially helpful if the show is not well known, and might include photocopies from books or magazines. Put in a photograph that can be used with the review, as well as your name and phone number, in case there is a question.

The Bad Seed

"One of our local papers has a reviewer who goes out of his way to pick on our productions," a reader told us. "He sometimes says things that just aren't true or, at best, shows his ignorance of the play or the playwright. He's been particularly hard on several of our actors, consistently singling them out for criticism. We don't get this treatment from other reviewers and we want to do something to stop it. But what? Can we ban a reviewer? If so, how?"

You can't really ban anyone from your theater, unless you have a restraining order—and judges only issue them when there is a clear and present physical danger involved. Even if you fail to invite this critic (we'll call him William Bligh) to review your show, he may still be assigned to do so by the editor—or he may request to do the review. Either way, an editor won't take kindly to your putting restrictions on the tickets you offer. He or she easily could retaliate by refusing to publicize your productions—and then paying for Bligh's tickets so he can write a review anyway.

We need to acknowledge our somewhat incestuous relationship with the media. We want publicity to help sell tickets and we bask in the warmth of good reviews. We complain when we don't get enough attention from the media, but we also resent criticism, even if it may be warranted.

We can't have it both ways, however. In exchange for the free publicity, we must accept the sometimes harsh spotlight of a critique. Be honest: Do you really want "fairness" and "accuracy" or kind words? When was the last time you protested to the paper when a critic was overly generous to one of your productions?

Some editors like complaints. They show that the reviewer is at least being read, and a controversial critic can be good for circulation. Above all, most editors believe a critic has a right to say whatever he or she honestly believes to be so. A review is, after all, an opinion—albeit a highly public one.

However, there are two critical failings you can protest with validity: one is consistent inaccuracy; the other is consistent use of negative words or phrases that belittle or demean and that are not germane to the production at hand. In both cases, the word *consistent* is important: You must show a pattern of poor performance.

We recall one critic who invariably fell asleep during performances and frequently did not return for the second act, yet who wrote his review as if he had been fully alert and present throughout. Such behavior could and should have been documented by the many theater companies this man reviewed. We also recall another critic who gave a new theater company overly kind reviews for far too long, excusing shoddy productions by referring to the company's persistence in the face of adversity. Such consistent bias, too, could have been easily documented.

Documenting the facts in the case is standard operating procedure for a reporter. So, if you plan to talk to the editor, first become an investigative reporter yourself. Start by collecting copies of all of Bligh's reviews during the last year or two. Use a yellow highlighter to emphasize particularly negative words or phrases referring to your productions; use a different color to highlight consistently positive remarks in other productions.

In both cases, look for patterns of expression that indicate bias. For example, Bligh may always refer to your company's play choices as being "over your head," while referring to another company's as "daring." Or he may damn you with faint praise by such descriptive words as "amateur," "unsophisticated," "adequate," "functional," and "safe," while characterizing another theater company as "nonprofessional," "no-nonsense," "basic," "distinctive," or "reliable." Be sure to compare his word choice with what he uses to describe another theater group of similar size, resources, and purpose. You can't expect an editor to sympathize if your community theater is described in different terms than a professional repertory company, for example.

If Bligh *consistently* pans your shows when other critics praise them, show this with a side-by-side listing of the comments—his versus theirs. Most editors won't excuse sloppy or inaccurate reporting. If Bligh often says things that "just aren't true," by all means report these as well, along with the correct information. Deal only in facts, however, not interpretation. If he frequently refers to your 500-seat theater as "cramped" and another company's 350-seat theater as "intimate," we think you have a strong case for bias. However, if he says your seats are "uncomfortable," that is an opinion more open to debate.

When you have documented your case of bias or inaccuracy or both, it's time to contact the editor. Don't go directly to the critic; you need a third party involved. As any good negotiator will tell you, avoid going in with demands. Instead, you are bringing information to light that you feel the editor needs to know. State your concerns and present hard evidence in the form of excerpts from reviews as explained previously. Show you understand the editor's viewpoint. Stress that you both want the same thing: even-handedness and accuracy. If you follow this approach, you should find that the editor will attempt to do something to correct the problem.

If you fear retaliation on the part of either the editor or the reviewer, you might consider having someone not connected with your company do the approaching—perhaps another member of the arts community. If you have a theater alliance in your area, an alliance representative can take on this role. A slightly different approach was the effort by one California organization, Theatre Bay Area. It added a section to its newsletter called *Press Check*, where a contributing writer, under the nom de plume "Punch," kept a watchful eye on the media—"nudging, nagging, lambasting if necessary, and giving praise where praise is due." The group's newsletter actively solicited readers to send in "clippings of anything you read in the press that's wrong-headed, erroneous, outrageous. Include your own personal comments, of course," it explained. "Don't worry, we'll guard your anonymity." (The idea of a "Press Check" is a good one, so long as it does not degenerate into petty sniping of its own.)

Finally, if you can't change the situation, learn to live with it. (And remember that—as you'll see in the next chapter—reviews may not be that important after all.) If a reviewer becomes a thorn in your side, remember that sometimes humor is the best medicine. We know one group who created an "award" given to the actor who in each production was the unlucky recipient of the sharp tongue of a local critic named Richard Simon. The award was a can of car wax, with a certificate commemorating that the actor had been "Simonized," and thereby honored as one of "a long and illustrious line of talented performers."

27 | "Never Heard of It"

What to Do When Your Show Isn't Well Known

NANCIANNE PFISTER

While there hasn't been any broad-based research on what draws an audience to a show, according to audience polls conducted by several arts organizations, word of mouth is the primary source of information. For example, in a poll taken by the Sacramento Area Regional Theatre Association (SARTA), more than half the respondents said they had heard of the production from another person. Direct mail and newspaper ads shared second place, with about 16 percent each. "Articles, posters, reviews, and telephone solicitations are either underused or have very little influence," according to the report.

Interestingly, people who say they do not attend theater regularly because they are not aware of productions are only half as likely to have heard about a particular show by direct mail. They are, along with people attending the theater for the first time, more reliant on word of mouth.

Fewer than five percent of the people surveyed gave reviews as a source of information about the show they were attending. Thus, despite some opinion to the contrary, reviews are clearly not an effective form of advertising. However, those already primed to go to a show may indeed use reviews as part of the decision-making process.

Other factors are involved in decision making as well. When asked what they wanted most from a play, audiences said "entertainment" first, followed by artistic quality and production quality. Plot and subject matter were deemed less important.

Interestingly, knowing someone in the production was mentioned frequently as a reason for attending a show. This is often why large-scale community productions draw crowds. Although the Sacramento results may differ slightly from those obtained in other cities, we suspect the SARTA poll is on the mark. (The SARTA survey, by the way, was conducted among 1,516 audience members at 36 different performances in 12 participating theaters.)

Advice from the Field

While a famous show almost sells itself, what kind of publicity campaign do you mount in order to sell a little-known offering?

Peter Massey, of Manatee Players Riverfront Theatre in Bradenton, Florida, agrees that this is always a challenge, especially since "we have a largely conservative audience and many retired people. We have to find some element that is marketable. When we chose *After the Fall*, we highlighted the relationship between its author, Arthur Miller, and Marilyn Monroe. We found that many in our audience knew *The Rainmaker*, so we advertised *110 in the Shade* as the musical version. We had a successful production of *Amadeus*, and *Lettice and Lovage* sold because it was written by the same author. If a show is completely foreign to us, we probably just would not do it."

When we talked with Marcia Harris, of South Carolina's Aiken Community Playhouse, she responded, "Funny you should ask, as we have an unfamiliar season. The only show people will know is *Nunsense*. We sell the other shows by relating them to things that people *do* know. *Dr. Cook's Garden*, for example, is an early Ira Levin play. Last year we did Levin's *Death Trap*, so there's a connection. *Remember My Name* is a French version of *The Diary of Anne Frank*. We linked it to the 50th anniversary of the end of World War II, and targeted veterans' groups in the area. One thing we did that was new to us was buy radio spots on a station that played big-band music. Our season members are in the 50 to 70 age group, just the people who would listen to that station. We have paid ads and a feature story in the paper. Sometimes, the theater gets a news story, as when Heartland Industries moved from here and gave us a storage building to auction as a fundraiser.

Most of all, our reputation is good, so word of mouth is our best advertising."

Publicizing a less well-known work is always a challenge, but especially in a small town, even though the town supports two dinner theaters and a children's theater, says Clara Hoover, of Clara N. Hoover Productions in Kingsport, Tennessee. "If we have a new show, we try to cast actors who are well known and well liked by our audiences. Paper advertising is usually not enough. We might take part of the show on the road, playing a scene at a Rotary meeting, for example. Then word of mouth helps us."

On the other side of the country, John Bouchard, of The Cast Adrift Players in Spokane, Washington, has an additional concern. Because shows are booked into clubs, the show must be entertaining and have no offensive language. "In this conservative community, there's always someone who will take exception to something," he points out. "We're a small group, with no real way to expand. Our best-received shows have been *Greater Tuna* and *Love Letters*. We get a newspaper listing the week before and try for an article about the show, which we never get. We mail out brochures, but mailing takes a lot of time, so we're planning a telephone tree for the next show."

Ginny Winsor, of Nebraska's Omaha Community Playhouse, advises publicity people to think creatively. "For *Queen of Bingo*, a remarkable show, we tied into the bingo subculture. We were *Bingo World's* whole newsletter. There was a contest and the winner came to Omaha and was taken by limousine to our opening night. We got permission to sell pickles during intermission. (No, not green, salty things, but rather pull-tab cards where you can win money.) In the script, someone wins a frozen turkey, so we got some turkeys donated to give to audience members. It's a major effort, but that's what it takes to promote a show no one knows."

It's not only patrons who have to be educated to this whole new world. Three actors and the director of *Queen of Bingo* spent a lot of time in bingo parlors, learning the body language—how to sit, how to daub your card—so they could do it right.

"Nobody wants to go to a show they never heard about," Winsor says. "We want patrons to come and enjoy it, so when word of mouth says what fun it is, they can say they saw it first."

Michael McKee, of Alabama's Mobile Theatre Guild, tells of a recent season in which almost all the shows were unknown in his community. "We anchored the season with *A Few Good Men*, a familiar title because of the film version. Then we related everything else to that show. Our season brochure headlined, 'A Few Good Men and A Few New Plays.' We did comparisons: "If you loved. . . , you'll love. . . ." The lack of familiarity did not deter our patrons. We got a good early response; of 200 season subscribers, 75 renewed their tickets in the first two weeks after the announcement of the season was released."

28 | *Did You Know?*

Don't Forget the Private Sector

In publicizing youth-theater classes or programs, we often overlook a large school-age population—private academies, special-needs classes, and home-schoolers. Parents of home-schooled children are often eager to have their youngsters participate in social and cultural groups such as a theater class, to broaden their experience in peer groups. Also, special-needs students who cannot be mainstreamed in regular academic classes may be perfectly suited to acting or design in workshop classes or performances. Private schools, both boarding and day schools, also often welcome the advantage of arts programs that their curriculum may not provide. An advantage for theater marketing and publicity directors is that the parents of these special students already have a communication network, usually a regular newsletter or bulletin. Remember this student population the next time you are budgeting for youth theater advertising and publicity. You might send a personal letter introducing your programs, then follow up with regular media releases and ads in their publications or school annuals.

History Lesson

Increase ticket sales by educating your audience about the historical or literary context of classic plays, or the background of plays that aren't well known. A subscriber or patron newsletter can do this very well, helping to interest potential playgoers who might not otherwise come—or help them explain the play to friends. For example, the *Callboard Companion* of the Omaha Community Playhouse (a 16-page publication that goes out to a large mailing list) recently spotlighted a dramatization of Willa Cather's *O Pioneers!* (set in nearby parts of Nebraska) with two articles on the novel and a third on how it was adapted for the Playhouse stage.

Making Connections

Look for logical tie-ins between your production and a local business. When one theater company presented the musical *Pump Boys and Dinettes*, set in a rural Southern truckstop, the local office of a major oil corporation sponsored the production and its gas stations promoted the play by offering customers coupons worth $1 off their admission. The theater, in turn, offered its patrons coupons worth $1 off full serve fill-ups at the gas station.

Looking Dated

Print the words *Dated Materials* on the front of your mailer to the left of the mail label area. Such wording gives your piece priority over bulk mail that does not have it.

That's the Ticket

Don't send tickets to reviewers; they are too easily lost in the confusion of the newsroom. Instead, ask them to phone to confirm they are coming. Then tell them where they are to pick up their tickets. Ask if they can use a photograph of the production; if they can, include one in the press kit. Make sure the photograph is fully captioned on the back side.

Working Together

The 19 professional theaters who comprise the New Jersey Theatre Group offered a three-play Theatre Sampler Series. For just $55, a theatergoer could choose any three plays from any of the theaters, thus creating his or her own mini-theater series. When a ticket order is received, the New Jersey Theatre Group sends vouchers with complete performance schedules for each of the three sampler selections. These vouchers are redeemable at each theater's box office—by mail or in person—for the best available seating on the first or second choice of performance dates. This is one of the finest examples we've seen of cooperation among theater companies, and working together this way makes for compelling public relations.

Final Thoughts

While the media have changed in significant ways in the past several decades, the purpose of publicity has changed very little. It's still a matter of informing people about your productions and motivating them to purchase tickets.

Whether you're dealing with newspapers, radio, television, direct mail, or the Internet, make your message strong enough to attract attention, simple enough to remember, and enticing enough to move the reader, viewer, or listener to action. That's the secret of good publicity.

The secret to success with media representatives is to learn to think like them. Know their needs, their likes and dislikes, and you'll do well. And always try to give them something exciting and new. Media outlets are always looking for something new, but an editor or reporter will never know unless you bring it to his or her attention.

And that's what publicity is all about, isn't it?

Contributors

CHRIS LANING lives in Davis, California, where she is a freelance writer, editor, designer, and publicist.

WYCLIFFE MCCRACKEN, now retired, spent a lifetime teaching, coaching, and writing drama.

SCOTT MILLER is founder and artistic director of St. Louis' New Line Theatre. His book, *The Director's Guide to the Musical Theatre*, was published in 1996 by Heinemann.

NEIL OFFEN is editor of *Stage Directions* magazine and has been a theater buff since his parents took him to see *South Pacific* on Broadway. He has been a sportswriter, news reporter, editor, freelance writer, news director, broadcaster, writer of a comic strip, and is the author or editor of ten published books.

STEPHEN PEITHMAN is editor-in-chief and one of the founders of *Stage Directions* magazine. At age 11, he wrote, directed, and starred in his own one-act plays and provided marionette shows to neighborhood friends. He has been an editor, public relations executive, college teacher, public information officer, theatrical director, and host of a weekly radio program devoted to musical theater.

NANCIANNE PFISTER is Associate Editor of *Stage Directions*.

MORE BOOKS
from Heinemann's *Stage Directions* series

Stage Directions Guide to Auditions
Edited by **Stephen Peithman** and **Neil Offen**

This book is different from other audition books in that it addresses the needs of both actors and directors. It offers expert advice on a range of topics, including choosing the right monologue, preparing your voice for auditions, steps to getting cast, sealing the deal at callbacks, publicizing auditions to get the right actors, paperwork to make auditions easier, preparing children for auditions, and narrowing down the casting choices.

0-325-00083-2 / 144pp / 1998

Stage Directions Guide to Directing
Edited by **Stephen Peithman** and **Neil Offen**

Every director—from the beginner to the most experienced—will find in this book invaluable information to make their direction more effective. Topics covered include things to look for in an audition, selecting the right play, criticizing effectively, basics of directing a musical, staging a big show with a small cast, blocking tips, managing rehearsals and schedules, and much more!

0-325-00112-X / 144pp est. / Available April 1999

Stage Directions Guide to Getting
and Keeping Your Audience
Edited by **Stephen Peithman** and **Neil Offen**

Today, theater competes with many forms of entertainment for people's leisure time. So how does a theater attract and maintain the audience it needs? You'll find out how in this book, discovering practical suggestions on advertising to motivate ticket-buyers, creating attention-getting mailings, using newsletters, numerous successful marketing and promotion tips, why audiences don't come, and much more!

0-325-00113-8 / 128pp est. / Available May 1999

Heinemann
TRADE

For more information about these books,
visit us on-line at **www.heinemanndrama.com**,
call 800-793-2154, fax 800-847-0938,
or write: Heinemann, Promotions Dept., 361 Hanover St., Portsmouth, NH 03801.